Nicholas Cooke

At the General Assembly of the Governor and Company of the Colony of Rhode-Island and Providence Plantations, etc.

Nicholas Cooke

At the General Assembly of the Governor and Company of the Colony of Rhode-Island and Providence Plantations, etc.

ISBN/EAN: 9783337183721

Printed in Europe, USA, Canada, Australia, Japan

Cover: Foto ©ninafisch / pixelio.de

More available books at **www.hansebooks.com**

June, 1776.

At the General Assembly of the Governor and Company of the Colony of *Rhode-Island* and *Providence Plantations,* in *New-England,* in *America,* begun and holden by Adjournment at *Newport,* within and for the said Colony, on the second *Monday* in *June,* in the Year of our Lord One Thousand Seven Hundred and Seventy-six.

PRESENT,

The Honorable

Nicholas Cooke, Esq;
GOVERNOR.

The Honorable

William Bradford, Esq; Deputy-Gov.

John Collins, Esq; Simeon Potter, Esq; John Jepson, Esq; James Arnold, jun. Esq; Jonathan Randall, Esq; William Potter, Esq; Thomas Church, Esq;	Assistants.

The SECRETARY.

DEPUTIES

DEPUTIES from the several TOWNS.
The Hon. METCALF BOWLER, *Esq; Speaker.*

NEWPORT:
Mr. John Wanton (*Son of Gideon*)
Mr. Samuel Fowler,
Col. George Sears,
Gideon Wanton, *Esq;*
Mr. Thomas Freebody,
Col. Joseph Belcher.

PROVIDENCE:
Col. Jonathan Arnold,
Mr. John Brown,
Mr. John Smith,
Col. Amos Atwell.

PORTSMOUTH:
Mr. Speaker,
Mr. Jonathan Cornell,
Mr. John Coddington,
Mr. John Thurston.

WARWICK:
William Greene, *Esq;*
Charles Holden, *Esq;*
Col. John Waterman.

WESTERLY:
Major-General Joshua Babcock,
Col. Joseph Noyes.

NEW-SHOREHAM:
Mr. Joshua Sands,
Mr. Edward Sands, *jun.*

NORTH-KINGSTOWN:
John Northup, *Esq;*
Major Sylvester Gardner.

SOUTH-KINGSTOWN:
Mr. Samuel Seagar,
Mr. Samuel Babcock.

EAST-GREENWICH:
Job Comstock, *Esq;*
Thomas Shippey, *Esq;*

JAMESTOWN:
Capt. Samuel Carr,
Benjamin Underwood, *Esq;*

SMITHFIELD:
Daniel Mowry, *jun. Esq;*
Capt. Andrew Waterman.

SCITUATE:
Mr. Christopher Potter.

GLOUCESTER.
C. I. Chad Brown.

CHARLESTOWN:
Capt. Joseph Stanton, *jun.*
Jonathan Hazard, *Esq;*

WEST-GREENWICH:
Thomas Tillinghast, *Esq;*
Judiah Aylesworth, *Esq;*

COVENTRY:
Ephraim Westcot, *Esq;*
Mr. Jeremiah Fenner.

EXETER:
George Peirce, *Esq;*

MIDDLETOWN:
Mr. Joshua Barker,
Mr. Nicholas Easton.

BRISTOL:
Shearjashub Bourn, *Esq;*
Col. Nathaniel Pearce.

TIVERTON:
Mr. Gideon Almy,
Col. John Cook.

LITTLE-COMPTON:
Capt. Thomas Brownel,
Mr. Daniel Wilbur.

WARREN:
Mr. Cromel Child,
Col. Sylvester Child.

CUMBERLAND:
John Dexter, *Esq;*
Capt. Elisha Waterman.

RICHMOND:
Major Richard Bailey.

CRANSTON:
Andrew Harris, *Esq;*
Zuriel Waterman, *Esq;*

HOPKINTON:
Mr. John Larkin,
Thomas Wells, *Esq;*

JOHNSTON:
Mr. John Fenner,
Peleg Williams, *Esq;*

NORTH-PROVIDENCE:
Major Thomas Olney,
Mr. Jonathan Jenckes, *jun.*

BARRINGTON:
Edward Bosworth, *Esq;*
Capt. Thomas Allen.

JOSIAS LYNDON, *Esq—Clerk of the Lower House.*

June, 1776.   57.

WHEREAS Mr. *Henry Peckham* exhibited an Account, by him charged against the Colony, for repairing Mr. *John Banister's* House: And the said Account being duly examined, *It is Voted and Resolved*, That the same be and hereby is allowed; and that *Seven Pounds Ten Shillings* Lawful Money, being the Amount thereof, be paid unto the said *Henry Peckham*, out of the General-Treasury.

<small>H. Peckham allowed £7. 10/.</small>

IT is *Voted and Resolved*, That the Persons at whose Houses the Piquet-Guard kept in *Middletown*, the Winter and Spring last past, be and they are hereby allowed *Twopence* Lawful Money *per* Night, for each and every Soldier, who kept at said Houses as a Piquet-Guard, during said Time: That the Owners of said Houses be accountable for what Wood they received of the Colony; and that the Money be paid by the Committee of Safety.

<small>Allowance to the Persons at whose Houses the Piquet-Guard was kept in *Middletown*.</small>

WHEREAS Messieurs *Metcalf Bowler*, *John Jenckes*, *Jabez Bowen*, *Thomas Greene*, and *John G. Wanton*, were appointed a Committee to audit the Accounts of *Joseph Clarke*, Esq; General-Treasurer; and they having presented to this Assembly the following State of his Account, and Report thereon, *to wit*:

<small>Report of the Committee who audited the Accounts of the General-Treasurer.</small>

Dr. The Colony of *Rhode-Island*, *&c.* with *Joseph Clarke*, Esq; General-Treasurer.

1776.
June. To Lawful Money Bills dated *May* 3, 1775, delivered the Committee and burnt,   £.7318 15 6
Interest on Ditto,   144 16 8¼
——————— £ 7463 12 2¼

To Lawful Money Bills of *June* 16, 1775, delivered the Committee and burnt,   3402 9 2
Interest on Ditto,   56 18 10½
——————— £ 3459 8 0¼
To

June, 1776.

To Lawful Money Bills of *June* 29, 1775, burnt,	£ 3833 15 10½			
Intereſt on Ditto,	60 13 11¾			
		£ 3894	9	10½
To 103 Treaſurer's Notes given for Old Tenor redeemed and burnt, Intereſt included,		1972	11	9
To 17 Treaſurer's Notes given for Lawful Money redeemed and burnt, Intereſt included,		325	11	11
To the Amount of Charges contained in my Book, kept in alphabetical Order, againſt the Colony,		23183	11	5
To Lawful Money Bills emitted *February* 1767,		1	18	6
To Ditto *March* 1766,		0	12	11
To Ditto *April* 1762,			5	0
To Intereſt on Ditto,		0	1	2¼
To a Lawful Money Bill, *Nov.* 1762, Old Tenor,	£ 33 0 0	0	0	3
To a Note given by *Thomas Richardſon*, Eſq;	£ 1 4 0			
To Intereſt on Ditto,	0 13 6¼			
		1	17	6¼
To Caſh paid *Metcalf Bowler*, Eſq; one of the Committee of Safety,	£ 11131	0	11
To Ditto paid *William Bradford*, Eſq; as Ditto,	3001	0	0
To Ditto paid *Stephen Mumford*, as Ditto,	2050	0	0
To Ditto paid *Daniel Tillinghaſt*, as Ditto,	8891	5	0
To Ditto paid *John Smith*, as Ditto,	11475	1	3
To Ditto paid *John Northup*, as Ditto,	4356	14	3
To Ditto paid *Jacob Greene*, as Ditto,	2331	12	0
To Ditto paid *John Cook*, as Ditto,	1440	16	0
To Ditto paid *Joſeph Stanton*, jun. as Ditto,	3699	4	0
To Ditto paid *Nathan Miller*, Eſq; Commiſſary,	14823	10	1
To Ditto paid *William Greene*, Eſq; to fit a Veſſel after Salt,	330	0	0
To Ditto paid *Metcalf Bowler*, Eſq; and *George Iriſh*, to fit a Veſſel after Salt,	500	0	0

To

June, 1776.

	£	s.	d.
To Ditto delivered the Infpectors of Salt-Petre,	539	17	4
To Ditto paid *Henry Ward*, Efq; from *Sept.* 1775, to *June* 5, 1776,	157	6	0
To Ditto paid *John Waterman*, towards the Powder-Mill,	50	0	0
To one Year's Salary, for my Service as Treafurer, from *May* 5, 1775, to *May* 1776,	50	0	
	105171	7	5¼
Balance due to the Colony, in Lawful Money.	19428	19	2¼
To Ditto in Old Tenor, £ 2556 5 1½			
£ 2589 5 1½	£ 124600	6	7½

1775.   Cr.

Nov. 6. By Balance due, as appears by Account audited *Sept.* 30, 1775, Ditto, in Old Tenor, £ 2589 5 1½   £ 4245   11   1½

17. By Cafh received of *Daniel Mowry*, Efq; for Stock fold at the Camp at *Cambridge*, the 6th Inft.   800   13   2¼

By Ditto of Col. *Daniel Hitchcock*, being Money overpaid by the Committee of Safety to the Soldiers in his Regiment,   52   2   6

1776.

Jan. 6. By Cafh received of *Nathaniel Mumford, Thomas Greene,* and *Gideon Mumford,* who were fent to *Philadelphia,* to bring the Continental Money from thence,   35760   0   8

14. By Cafh received of *Nathaniel Mumford,* which he received at *Philadelphia,* on General *Hopkins's* Order,   250   0   0

18. By Ditto received from *Jofeph Hoxfie,* per the Hands of *James Congdon,* 3d, in Part of the Sale of Sheep carried from *New-Shoreham* to *Charleftown,*   103   9   4½

B   By

June, 1776.

	£	s	d
By Ditto received of Dr. *Babcock* and Company, for Sheep fold by them, brought from *New-Shoreham*,	39	10	0
Feb. 6. By Ditto received of *James Hill*, for Goods, formerly the Property of *Gilbert Deblois*, as per two Receipts,	639	4	2
19. By Ditto received of *James Congdon*, 3d, on Account of *Joseph Hoxsie*, for Sale of Sheep in *Charlystown*, brought from *New-Shoreham*,	39	17	2
By Ditto received the 6th Instant, in Silver and Gold, from *William Rhodes*, per the Hands of Mr. *John Jenckes*,	610	4	6
Mar. 11. By Cash received of *George Irish*, in Gold, to supply the Army at *Quebec*,	188	18	0
14. By Ditto received of Col. *Thomas Church*,	613	10	0
16. By Ditto received from *William Potter*, by the Hands of *Ambrose Page*, Esq;	82	0	0
17. By Ditto received of *James Hill*, for Goods formerly the Property of *Gilbert Deblois*,	342	2	3
28. By Ditto received of *Stephen Mumford*, Esq; for the Use of the Army at *Quebec*,	20	15	4½
Apr. 10. By Ditto received of *Metcalf Bowler*, Esq; in Gold, for Ditto,	131	9	1
16. By Ditto received of *James Congdon*, 3d, for Ditto,	2	17	6
By Ditto received from *Joseph Hoxsie*, per the Hands of *James Congdon*, 3d, on Account of Sheep from *Luck-Island*,	7	12	3½
By Cash received of *Stephen Mumford*, Esq; for the Use of the Army at *Quebec*,	30	0	0
May 6. By Ditto received of *Josias Lyndon*, Esq; for Ditto,	12	10	0

By

By Ditto received of *Peter Phillips*, Efq; for Guns, appraifed in Col. *Varnum's* Regiment,	422	0	0
May 11. By Ditto received of *Metcalf Bowler*, Efq; for the Supply of the Army at *Quebec*,	90	1	0
13. By Ditto received of Col. *Daniel Tillinghaft*, for Ditto,	5	14	0
14. By Ditto received of *Jofeph Clarke*, Efq; for Ditto,	30	0	0
27. By Ditto received of *James Hill*, for Goods formerly the Property of *Gilbert Deblois*,	80	0	0
1775.			
Oct. 31. By Lawful Money Bills emitted at *Providence*,	20000	0	0
1776.			
Jan. 8. By Ditto emitted at Ditto,	40000	0	0
Mar. 18. By Ditto emitted at *Eaft-Greenwich*,	20000	0	0
	£ 12,600	6	1½

We the Subfcribers, with *Metcalf Bowler*, Efq; being appointed a Committee to audit the Accounts of the General-Treafurer, do report, that we find a Balance of Nineteen Thoufand Four Hundred and Twenty-eight Pounds Nineteen Shillings and Two-pence One Farthing Lawful Money; and the Sum of Two Thoufand Five Hundred and Eighty-nine Pounds Five Shillings and One Penny Halfpenny Old Tenor, due to the Colony, agreeable to the above Account.

      JOHN JENCKES,
      JABEZ BOWEN,
      THOMAS GREENE,
      JOHN G. WANTON.

Providence, May 31, 1776.

And the Premifes being duly confidered, *It is Voted and Refolved*, That the faid Report be and hereby is accepted.

          WHEREAS

J. Greene's Account audited.

WHEREAS Meſſieurs *Nathaniel Mumford, Thomas Greene,* and *Gideon Mumford,* were appointed a Committee to audit the Accounts of *Jacob Greene,* Eſq; one of the Committee of Safety ; and they having preſented to this Aſſembly the following State of his Account, and the Report thereon, *to wit :*

Dr. *Jacob Greene,* Eſq; one of the Committee of Safety, to the Colony of *Rhode-Iſland.*

1776.
May 25. To Amount of Caſh you received of the General-Treaſurer, *per* his Certificate dated *May* 25, £2331 12 0
To Amount of ſundry Deductions,   80 8 6¼
                                  ─────────────
                                  2412 0 6¾
Balance due to *Jacob Greene,*   377 19 2¼
                                  ─────────────
                                  2789 19 9

1776.   Cr.
May 25. By Amount of your Account,   840 11 5½
By Amount of one other Account,   181 19 8
By Amount of your other Account, for
  Two Field-Pieces,   74 16 5
By Amount of the Muſter-Roll of Capt. *Job*
  Peirce's Company,   661 13 0
By Ditto Capt. *Thomas Gorton*'s Company,   369 4 4
By Ditto Capt. *Joſiah Gibbs*'s Company,   392 14 3
By Amount of Account of *Nathaniel Greene*
  and Company,   53 3 4
By Amount of Galley *Waſhington*'s Account, 186 11 3½
                                            ─────────────
                                            2760 13 9
By Commiſſions on £500 at 1½ *per Cent.*   7 10 0
By Commiſſions on £2260 13 9
  at 1 *per Cent.*
Deduct   80 8 6
                 ─────────
                 £2180 5 3
                 at 1 *per Cent.*   21 16 0
                                            ─────────────
Eaſt-Greenwich, May 25, 1776.
Errors excepted, for *Jacob Greene,*   £2789 19 9
          Per WILLIAM GREENE.

Dr.

Dr. *Jacob Greene*, Esq; his Account Current with
the Colony of *Rhode-Island*.
1776.
May 25. To Amount of Cash you received of the
General-Treasurer, on Account of Outfits, Cargo and Loss of the Sloop *Maryland*, for Salt, as *per* Certificate from the Treasurer of this Date, £ 435 0 0

Balance due to *Jacob Greene*, 10 14 13

£ 445 14 10

1776. Cr.
May. By Amount of your Account for Cargo and Outfits of the Sloop *Maryland*, for Salt, £ 185 1 4

By Amount of the Value of said Sloop (taken by a Man of War) as appraised by Col. *Richard Fry*, and Mr. *Robert Stevens*, which appears by the Charter-Party, 255 0 0

By Three Months Interest on £ 255, from Commencement of the Charter-Party, *Jan.* 24, 1776, to *April* 24th following, being the Time of the Captain's Arrival home, as *per* Agreement in Charter-Party, 3 16 6

By Commissions on £ 185 1 s. 4 d. at 1 *per Cent.* 1 17 0

East-Greenwich, *May* 25, 1776.

Errors excepted for *Jacob Greene*, £ 445 14 10
Per WILLIAM GREENE.

THIS 25th of *May*, *A. D.* 1776, we carefully examined and finished all the above Accounts.
NATHANIEL MUMFORD,
THOMAS GREENE,
GIDEON MUMFORD.

MEMORANDUM. *William Sweet*, jun. Captain of the Sloop *Maryland*, saved the Cash which he carried out with him, and brought it home, amounting to *One Hundred and Seventy-five Dollars*.

AND the said Premises being duly considered, *It is Voted and Resolved*, That the said Report be and
hereby

hereby is accepted; and that the Balance mentioned therein, being *Three Hundred and Eighty-eight Pounds Fourteen Shillings and One Farthing* Lawful Money, be paid unto the said *Jacob Greene*, out of the General-Treasury.

W. Greene to pay £38 11s. 6d.

WHEREAS *William Greene*, Esq; did sell and dispose of 2939 lb. Weight of Hides upon the Colony's Account, which amounted to *Thirty-eight Pounds Eleven Shillings and Sixpence* Lawful Money: *It is Voted and Resolved*, That the said *William Greene* be and he is hereby directed to pay the aforesaid Sum into the General-Treasury.

R. Peckham allowed £3 5s. 6d.

WHEREAS Mrs. *Ruth Peckham* exhibited unto this Assembly an Account, by her charged against the Colony, for boarding and nursing *George Hamilton*, a wounded Prisoner, taken at *Prudence*: And the said Account being duly examined, *It is Voted and Resolved*, That the same be and hereby is allowed; and that *Three Pounds Five Shillings and Sixpence* Lawful Money, being the Amount thereof, be paid unto the said *Ruth Peckham*, out of the General-Treasury.

W. Greenman to receive the Wages of his Son, who is a Minor.

WHEREAS Mr. *William Greenman* preferred his Petition to this Assembly, setting forth, that his Son, *Wilson Greenman*, being about eighteen Years of Age, in the Month of *October, A. D.* 1775, inlisted as a Minute-Man, under Capt. *Andrew Waterman*, and served as such upon *Rhode-Island*, until about the Eighth Day of *December, A. D.* 1775, when he was discharged by the said Captain: That his said Son, being a Minor, he the said *William* is entitled to receive one Half Part of his Wages: That the said Capt. *Waterman* refuses to pay the same; and that on the Tenth Day of said *December*, the said *Wilson* was taken and carried on board one of the King's Ships, where he is now detained as a Prisoner: And thereupon the said *William* prayed this Assembly to order and direct the said Capt. *Waterman* to pay the whole of said Wages to him, or such Part as this Assembly should think meet.

WHEREUPON

WHEREUPON this Assembly taking the Premises into Consideration, *Do Vote and Resolve,* That Capt. *Andrew Waterman* pay unto the Petitioner *(William Greenman)* all the Wages that now remain due and unpaid, for the said *Wilson's* Services.

IT is *Voted and Resolved,* That Messieurs *Nathaniel Blumford, Thomas Greene,* and *Gideon Mumford,* be and they are hereby directed to make Enquiry what Salt is in the Colony, belonging to the Government, and what the same cost, including the Vessels and Cargoes which were lost, as well as those which returned safe; and make Report to this Assembly by *Friday* Morning next, at farthest. — Committee to enquire what Salt is in the Government.

IT is *Voted and Resolved,* That the Sheriff of the County of *Newport* do, and he is hereby directed to take immediate Possession of the Tan-Yard, Vats, Leather, Stock of Hides, and every thing else in the Tan-Yard in *Newport* belonging to *George Rome,* for the Use of the Colony. — Sheriff of *Newport* to take Possession of *G Rome's* Tan Yard, &c.

WHEREAS Mrs. *Mary Gwin* exhibited to this Assembly an Account, by her charged against the Colony, for nursing *George Hamilton,* a wounded Prisoner, taken at *Prudence*; and for lodging Soldiers: And the said Account being duly examined, *It is Voted and Resolved,* That the same be and hereby is allowed; and that *Eleven Shillings and One Penny Halfpenny* Lawful Money, being the Amount thereof, be paid to the said *Mary Gwin,* out of the General-Treasury. — M. Gwin allowed 11/1½

IT is *Voted and Resolved,* That Mr. *Cromel Child* be and he is hereby directed to make suitable wooden Wheels to the Ship Gun-Carriages he is employed to make for the Colony; and that Mr. *Edward Church* make such Wheels for the Carriages he is employed to make for the Colony. — Wheels ordered for Gun-Carriages.

IT is *Voted and Resolved,* That Capt. *William Sweet,* jun. do and he is hereby directed to pay into the Gene-

W. Sweet, jun. to pay 175 Dollars into the General-Treasury.

neral-Treasury the Sum of *One Hundred and Seventy-five Dollars,* now in his Hands belonging to the Colony: That the General-Treasurer apply to said *Sweet* for the same; and in case of Neglect or Refusal, sue for the same to the then next Inferior Court in the Colony.

J. Lafell allowed £18.

WHEREAS Mr. *John Lafell*, of *Providence*, preferred his Petition to this Assembly, setting forth, That he was appointed to ride Post from *Providence* to *New-London*, for One Year, at the Price of *One Hundred and Eighty-five Dollars*: That being so appointed, he purchased two Horses, and otherwise equipt himself for the said Service: That he performed the same with Care and Fidelity for the Space of Three Months, when he was superseded by Mr. *Benjamin Mumford*, who was appointed by *William Goddard*, Esq; Surveyor of the Post-Offices: That the Petitioner has sustained considerable Damage by the Expence of equipping himself in Manner as aforesaid: Wherefore he besought this Assembly to consider the same, and grant him such a Sum to compensate for his Damages sustained as should seem meet: Whereupon this Assembly appointed Messieurs *Nathaniel Mumford, Thomas Greene,* and *Gideon Mumford,* to enquire into the Premises, who made the following Report: "We have "made careful Enquiry into the subject Matter of the "above Petition, and from the best Information we can "get concerning it, are of Opinion, that the Damage "sustained by the Petitioner is equal to *Eighteen Pounds* "Lawful Money, which Sum we think he is entitled "to." And the same being duly considered, *It is Voted and Resolved,* That the above Report be and hereby is accepted; and that the aforesaid Sum of *Eighteen Pounds* Lawful Money be paid unto the said *John Lafell,* out of the General-Treasury.

W. Greene's Accounts settled.

WHEREAS Messieurs *Nathaniel Mumford, Thomas Greene,* and *Gideon Mumford,* were appointed a Committee to audit the Accounts of *William Greene,* Esq; who fitted out a Vessel to purchase Salt for the Colony; and they having presented unto this Assembly the Accounts of the said *William Greene,* with the following State thereof, and Report thereon, *to wit:*

June, 1776.

Dr. *William Greene*, Efq; his Account with the Colony of *Rhode-Ifland.*

1776.
May 25. To Amount of Cafh you received of the General-Treafurer, as *per* Account, to wit:

				£	s	d
Jan. 19. Cafh,	—	—		200	0	0
May 14. Ditto,	—	—		130	0	0
				330	0	0
To Cafh you received of Capt. *Cafey*,				62	14	7
			£	392	14	7

1776. Cr.
May 25. By Amount of your Account of Cargo and Outfits of Schooner *Abigail*, and Amount of Portage Bill, and inward Charges, £ 314 11 4½

By Amount of your Commiffions on the above Sum, at 1 *per Cent.* 3 3 0

Balance due to the Colony, 75 0 2¼

Eaft-Greenwich, May 25, 1776. £ 392 14 7.
Errors excepted,
Per WILLIAM GREENE.

THIS 25th of *May*, 1776, we carefully examined the above mentioned Account, and ftated as above.

NATHANIEL MUMFORD,
THOMAS GREENE,
GIDEON MUMFORD.

AND the faid Premifes being duly confidered, *It is Voted and Refolved,* That the faid Report be and is hereby accepted; and that the Balance mentioned therein, being *Seventy-five Pounds and Twopence Halfpenny* Lawful Money, be paid by the faid *William Greene,* into the General-Treafury.

WHEREAS Meffieurs *Nathaniel Mumford, Thomas Greene,* and *Gideon Mumford,* who were appointed a Committee

Report upon J. Smith's Account.

D

Committee to audit the Account of Mr. *John Smith* one of the Committee of Safety, presented unto this Assembly the Account of Particulars charged by the said *John Smith*, and also the following general State thereof, *to wit:*

Dr. *John Smith*, Esq; his Account Current with the Colony of *Rhode-Island.*

1776.
Feb. 7. To Amount of Cash you received of the General-Treasurer, as *per* Certificate, £ 5350   1   3
To an Overcharge in Account,   1   4   3

            5351   5   6
Balance due to *John Smith*,   13 17   6

            5365   3   0

1776.   Cr.
Feb. 7. By Amount of your Account within, £ 5365   3   0
    Providence, *February* 7, 1776.
       Errors excepted,
          Per JOHN SMITH.

THIS 7th Day of *February*, settled and adjusted the above Account.
       NATHANIEL MUMFORD,
       THOMAS GREENE,
       GIDEON MUMFORD.

AND the Premises being duly considered, *It is Voted and Resolved*, That the aforegoing Report be and the same is hereby accepted; and that *Thirteen Pounds Seventeen Shillings and Sixpence* Lawful Money, being the Balance therein mentioned, be paid the said *John Smith*, out of the General-Treasury.

J. Jenckes's Account adjusted.   WHEREAS Messieurs *Nathaniel Mumford, Thomas Greene,* and *Gideon Mumford*, were appointed a Committee to audit the Account of Mr. *John Jenckes*, for fitting out the Sloops *Liberty, Diamond,* and *Sally,* for warlike Stores for the Colony: And they having presented unto this Assembly the Account of Particulars of the said *John Jenckes*, and the following State of his Account, and Report thereon, *to wit:*
                   Dr.

June, 1776.

Dr. *John Jenckes,* Esq; his Account Current with the Colony of *Rhode-Island.*

1776.
Jan. 13. To Cash you received of the General-Treasurer, *per* his Certificate, £3811 13 6
To Amount of 100 Barrels of Flour charged by *John Smith,* 186 4 6
Balance due to *John Jenckes,* 462 11 5¼

£4460 9 5¼

1776.   Cr.
Jan. 13. By Amount of Cargo and Outfits of the Sloop *Liberty, Christopher Whipple,* Master, £1011 5 6
By Amount of your Account of the Cargo and Outfits of Sloop *Diamond, Samuel Sowle,* Master, 2568 16 10
By Amount of your Account of Cargo and Outfits of Sloop *Sally, Nathaniel Packard,* Master, 880 7 1¾

Providence, February 13, 1776. £4460 9 5¼
Errors excepted,
Per JOHN JENCKES.

Providence, February 13, 1776. Then settled and adjusted the above Account, by Order of the Honorable the General Assembly.

NATHANIEL MUMFORD,
THOMAS GREENE,
GIDEON MUMFORD.

AND the said Premises being duly considered, *It is Voted and Resolved,* That the said Report be and hereby is accepted; and that the Balance mentioned therein, being *Four Hundred and Sixty-two Pounds Eleven Shillings and Fivepence One Farthing* Lawful Money, be paid unto the said *John Jenckes,* out of the General-Treasury.

WHEREAS Col. *Joseph Belcher* exhibited unto this Assembly an Account, by him charged against the Colony, for Copper-Ware and other Necessaries supplied the Row-Galley *Spitfire* with, and also for divers Articles

J. Belcher allowed £7 1*s.* 8*d.*

for

for the Use of the Soldiery: And the said Account being duly examined, *It is Voted and Resolved,* That the same be and hereby is allowed; and that *Seven Pounds One Shilling and Eightpence* Lawful Money, being the Amount thereof, be paid to said *Joseph Belcher,* out of the General-Treasury.

J. G. Wanton, J. Jenckes, J. Bowen, and T. Greene, allowed £9 6s.

WHEREAS Messieurs *John G. Wanton, John Jenckes, Jabez Bowen,* and *Thomas Greene,* exhibited unto this Assembly an Account, by them charged against the Colony, for their Time and Trouble in settling the Accounts of the General-Treasurer: And the said Account being duly examined, *It is Voted and Resolved,* That the same be and hereby is allowed; and that the Amount thereof, being *Nine Pounds Six Shillings,* be paid to them in the following Manner, *to wit:* To Mr. *John G. Wanton, Four Pounds Four Shillings,* Mr. *John Jenckes, Thirty Shillings,* Mr. *Jabez Bowen, Thirty Shillings,* Mr. *Thomas Greene, Two Pounds Two Shillings,* out of the General-Treasury.

Sheriff of Newport to take Possession of G. Rome's Estate in Newport.

IT is Voted and Resolved, That the Sheriff of the County of *Newport* do and he is hereby directed to take immediate Possession of a Lot of Land, with two Dwelling-Houses thereon, lying in *Newport,* on the south Side of the Parade, being the Estate of *George Rome,* to and for the Use of the Colony: That the said Sheriff likewise take into his Possession, for the Use of the Colony, all other the Estate of the said *George Rome,* lying in the County of *Newport,* which hath not already been seized: And that the Tenants of the Estate aforesaid account for all Arrearages of Rent to the Colony.

Report upon D. Tillinghast's Account.

WHEREAS Messieurs *Nathaniel Mumford, Thomas Greene,* and *Gideon Mumford,* who were appointed a Committee to audit the Account of *Daniel Tillinghast,* Esq; one of the Committee of Safety, with the Colony, presented unto this Assembly the Account of Particulars, charged by the said *Daniel Tillinghast,* and also the following general State of his Account, *to wit:*

Dr.

June, 1776.

Dr. Col. *Daniel Tillinghast,* his Account Current with the Colony of *Rhode-Island.*

1776.		£	s.	d.
Jan. 11. To Cash you received of the General-Treasurer, as *per* Certificate,		2265	0	0
To Amount of sundry Errors in charging and casting,		36	17	10½
Balance due to *Daniel Tillinghast,*		105	10	7½
		£2407	8	6

1776. Cr.	£	s.	d.
Jan. 11. By Amount of your Account,	2376	3	1½
By Commissions on £1500, at 1½ *per Cent.*	22	10	0
By Commissions on £876, at 1 *per Cent.*	8	15	4½
	£2407	8	6

Providence, February 11, 1776.
Errors excepted,
Per DANIEL TILLINGHAST.

Providence, February 11, 1776. Then settled and adjusted the above Account.
NATHANIEL MUMFORD,
THOMAS GREENE,
GIDEON MUMFORD.

AND the aforesaid Premises being duly considered, *It is Voted and Resolved,* That the aforesaid Report be and the same is hereby accepted; and that *One Hundred and Five Pounds Ten Shillings and Sevenpence Halfpenny* Lawful Money, being the Balance of the aforesaid Account, be paid the said *Daniel Tillinghast,* out of the General-Treasury.

WHEREAS Messieurs *Nathaniel Mumford,* and *Thomas Greene,* who were appointed a Committee to audit the Accounts of *John Northup,* Esq; with the Colony, as one of the Committee of Safety; and for fitting out the Brigantine *Nancy,* to procure Salt for the Colony, laid before this Assembly an Account of the Particulars charged by the said *John Northup,* and also the following general State of his Account, *to wit:*
E.   Dr.

Report upon *J. Northup's* Account.

June, 1776.

Dr. *John Northup*, Esq; one of the Committee of Safety, to the Colony of *Rhode-Island*.

1776.				
May 25.	To Amount of Cash your received of the General-Treasurer, as *per* his Certificate,	£4356	14	3
	To Amount of sundry Deductions made,	2	9	10
	To Amount of your Account of Credit for Tallow, &c. as *per* your Account given in,	8	1	3
	Balance due to *John Northup*,	120	16	1¼
		£4488	1	5¾

1776.	Cr.			
May 25.	By Amount of your Account from the 29th of *November*, 1775, to *Jan*. 16, 1776, as *per* Account,	£843	0	0
	By Amount of your Account to this Day,	3274	12	1¼
	By Amount of the Balance due on the Brigantine *Nancy*'s Outfits and Charges, for Salt, as *per* Account adjusted,	325	1	6¼
	By Commissions on £843, at 1½ *per Cent*.	12	12	10
	By Ditto on £3274 12 1¼ at 1 *per Cent*.	32	14	11
		£4488	1	5

East-Greenwich, May 25, 1776.
Errors excepted,
Per JOHN NORTHUP.

THIS 25th Day of *May* settled and adjusted the above Account.

NATHANIEL MUMFORD,
THOMAS GREENE.

AND the Premises being duly considered, *It is Voted and Resolved*, That the aforesaid Balance of *One Hundred and Twenty Pounds Sixteen Shillings and One Penny Farthing* Lawful Money, be paid the said *John Northup*, out of the General-Treasury: That he pay into the General-Treasury the Sum of *Thirty-seven Pounds Four Shillings* Lawful Money, in Gold, being so much brought in the said Brigantine *Nancy*, and receive Lawful Money Bills in Lieu thereof, the General Treasurer allowing

June, 1776.

allowing him for the Loss of Weight in the Gold; and that he sell to the best Advantage all the Goods remaining in his Hands belonging to the Colony, excepting a Quantity of Duck, two Muskets and two Blunderbusses, which are to be put on board the Row-Gallies.

WHEREAS Major *Richard Bailey* purchased for the Use of the Town of *Richmond* a Quantity of Lead; which being duly examined into, *It is Voted and Resolved,* That the said Major *Richard Bailey* be and he is hereby allowed the Sum of *Four Pounds Ten Shillings and Fourpence* Lawful Money, being the Sum he paid for said Lead; and that the Sum aforesaid, be paid unto the said Major *Richard Bailey,* out of the General-Treasury.

R. Bailey allowed £ 4 10 s. 4 d.

WHEREAS Mr. *Seth Snell* exhibited to this Assembly three several Accounts, by him charged against the Colony, for Blacksmith's Work done in and about the Row Gallies *Washington* and *Spitfire :* Which Accounts being duly examined, *It is Voted and Resolved,* That the same be and hereby are allowed; and that *Fifteen Pounds and Fourpence* Lawful Money, being the Amount thereof, be paid unto the said *Seth Snell,* out of the General-Treasury.

S. Snell allowed £ 15 4 d.

AN Account being laid before this Assembly by Mr. *Philip Acklin,* for the Service of himself, and the Use of his Boat, &c. in carrying Col. *Richmond* and other Officers from *Newport* to *East-Greenwich :* Which said Account being duly examined, *It is Voted and Resolved,* That the same be and hereby is allowed; and that *Two Pounds Four Shillings and Sixpence* Lawful Money, being the Amount thereof, be paid unto the said *Philip Acklin,* out of the General-Treasury.

P. Acklin allowed £ 2 4 s. 6 d.

WHEREAS Mr. *Joshua Coggeshall* exhibited to this Assembly an Account, by him charged against the Colony, for supplying the Soldiers with Victuals, and keeping Oxen and Horses that were employed in Government Service : Which said Account being duly examined, *It is Voted and Resolved,* That the same be and hereby

J. Coggeshall allowed £ 3 16 s.

June, 1776.

hereby is allowed; and that *Three Pounds Sixteen Shillings* Lawful Money, being the Amount thereof, be paid unto the said *Joshua Coggeshall,* out of the General-Treasury.

W. Richmond allowed £3 5d.

An Account being laid before this Assembly, by Col. *William Richmond,* for Cash paid for his Expences and Horse-hire to *Providence* and *East-Greenwich,* to attend the Assembly, by Order of his Honor the Governor: Which Account being duly examined, *It is Voted and Resolved,* That the same be and hereby is allowed; and that *Three Pounds and Fivepence,* being the Balance thereof, be paid unto the said *William Richmond,* out of the General-Treasury.

C. Olney allowed £3 15s. 4d.

Whereas Major *Christopher Olney* exhibited unto this Assembly three several Accounts, by him charged against the Colony, for Horse-hire and Expences, in attending the General Assembly, by Order of his Honor the Governor: Which said Accounts being duly examined, *It is Voted and Resolved,* That the same be and hereby are allowed; and that *Three Pounds Fifteen Shillings and Fourpence* Lawful Money, being the Amount of said Accounts, be paid unto the said *Christopher Olney,* out of the General-Treasury.

G. Westcot allowed £1 1s. 3d.

An Account being laid before this Assembly by *George Westcot,* for Oars for a Whaleboat belonging to the Colony: Which being duly examined, *It is Voted and Resolved,* That the same be and hereby is allowed; and that *One Pound One Shilling and Threepence* Lawful Money be paid unto the said *George Westcot,* out of the General-Treasury.

A. Anthony allowed £2 19s. 9d.

An Account being laid before this Assembly by Mr. *Abraham Anthony,* for victualling and lodging the *Pawtuxet Rangers,* while upon Alarm at *Warwick Neck:* Which being duly examined, *It is Voted and Resolved,* That the same be and hereby is allowed; and that the Amount thereof, being *Two Pounds Nineteen Shillings and Ninepence* Lawful Money, be paid unto the said *Abraham Anthony,* out of the General-Treasury.

An

June, 1776.

An Account charged againſt the Colony by Mr. *W. Palmer Walter Palmer,* for the Expences of a Boat and Hands to carry Major *Olney* to *Eaſt-Greenwich,* where they were detained by the Weather, being laid before and duly examined by this Aſſembly, *It is Voted and Reſolved,* That *One Pound Five Shillings and Ninepence* Lawful Money be allowed the ſaid *Walter Palmer,* in full Satisfaction for the ſaid Account; and that the ſame be paid him, out of the General-Treaſury.

allowed £ 1 5 *s.* 9 *d.*

An Account charged againſt the Colony by Dr. *Peter T. Wales,* for Medicines and Attendance upon two ſick Soldiers in the Colony's Brigade, being laid before and duly examined by this Aſſembly, *It is Voted and Reſolved,* That the ſame be and hereby is allowed; and that *Three Pounds Twelve Shillings and Eightpence* Lawful Money, being the Amount thereof, be paid the ſaid *Peter T. Wales,* out of the General-Treaſury.

P. T. Wales allowed £ 3 12 *s.* 8 *d.*

An Account charged againſt the Colony by Mr. *J. Newton John Newton,* for a Cedar Boat and Oars taken by General *Hopkins* for the Uſe of the Colony, having been laid before and duly examined by this Aſſembly, *It is Voted and Reſolved,* That the ſame be and hereby is allowed; and that *Six Pounds Ten Shillings* Lawful Money, being the Amount thereof, be paid the ſaid *John Newton,* out of the General-Treaſury.

allowed £ 6 10 *s.*

An Account charged againſt the Colony by Mr. *A. Lockwood Amos Lockwood,* for Proviſions ſupplied by him to the Troops on *Warwick* Neck, having been laid before and duly examined by this Aſſembly, *It is Voted and Reſolved,* That the ſame be and hereby is allowed; and that *Nine Shillings and Twopence One Farthing* Lawful Money, being the Amount thereof, be paid the ſaid *Amos Lockwood,* out of the General-Treaſury.

allowed 9 *s.* 2 *d.* ¼

An Account charged by Mr. *Aaron Chaſe* againſt the Colony, for freighting Stock and Grain from *Prudence* to the main Land, having been laid before and duly examined by this Aſſembly, *It is Voted and Reſolved,* That the ſame be and hereby is allowed; and that *To. e. Pounds Thirteen Shillings and Threepence* Lawful Money,

A. Chaſe allowed £ 3 13 *s.* 5 *d.*

F

76 *June,* 1776.

Money, being the Amount thereof, be paid the said *Aaron Chafe*, out of the General-Treasury.

G. B. *Allen* allowed £7 2s. ¾
An Account charged by Mr. *George B. Allen* against the Colony, for freighting Hay and Grain from *Prudence* to the main Land, having been laid before and duly examined by this Assembly, *It is Voted and Resolved*, That the same be and hereby is allowed; and that *Seven Pounds Two Shillings and Three Farthings* Lawful Money, being the Amount thereof, be paid to the said *George B. Allen*, out of the General-Treasury.

B *Peirce* allowed £2 2s. 6d.
An Account charged by Capt. *Benjamin Peirce* against the Colony, for his Horse-hire and Expences in going from *Newport* to *Providence*, being summoned to attend the Trial of Col. *Henry Babcock*, having been laid before and duly examined by this Assembly, *It is Voted and Resolved*, That *Two Pounds Two Shillings and Sixpence* Lawful Money be allowed, and paid the said *Benjamin Peirce*, out of the General-Treasury, which shall be in full Satisfaction of the said Account.

S. *Child* allowed £1 3s.
An Account charged by Col. *Sylvester Child* against the Colony, for the Expences of removing *George Hamilton*, a wounded Prisoner, belonging to the *British* Navy, from *Warren* to *Newport*, in order to exchange him, having been laid before and duly examined by this Assembly, *It is Voted and Resolved*, That the same be and hereby is allowed; and that *One Pound Three Shillings* Lawful Money, being the Amount thereof, be paid the said *Sylvester Child*, out of the General-Treasury.

J. *Bliven* allowed 10s.
IT is Voted and Resolved, That *Ten Shillings* Lawful Money be allowed and paid to Mr. *James Bliven*, out of the General-Treasury, for the Damage done to a Gun, received by him of Mr. *Augustus Saunders*, for the Use of the Colony.

S. *Aborn* allowed 9s.
An Account charged by Mr. *Samuel Aborn* against the Colony, for his Services in removing Stock from the Islands to the main Land, by Order of his Honor the

June, 1776.

the Governor, having been laid before and duly examined by this Assembly, *It is Voted and Resolved*, That the same be and hereby is allowed; and that *Nine Shillings* Lawful Money, being the Amount thereof, be paid the said *Samuel Aborn*, out of the General-Treasury.

An Account charged by *Charles Tillinghast*, Esq; against the Colony, for his Services in removing the Stock and Hay from *Jamestown*, and for divers Expences attending that Business, by him paid, having been laid before and duly examined by this Assembly, *It is Voted and Resolved*, That the same be and hereby is allowed; and that *Twenty four Pounds Sixteen Shillings and One Penny* Lawful Money, being the Balance due thereon, be paid the said *Charles Tillinghast*, out of the General-Treasury.

C. Till'nghast allowed £ 24 16 s. 1 d.

An Account charged by *Richard Smith*, Esq; Sheriff of the County of *Bristol*, for warning the Members of the General Assembly in the County aforesaid, to attend at the Session held at *East-Greenwich* in *March* last, having been laid before and duly examined by this Assembly, *It is Voted and Resolved*, That the same be and hereby is allowed; and that *Twelve Shillings* Lawful Money, being the Amount thereof, be paid the said *Richard Smith*, out of the General-Treasury.

R. Smith allowed 12 s.

An Account charged against the Colony by Mr. *Anthony Low*, for billeting Part of Capt. *Thomas Rice's* Company, when upon actual Duty, having been laid before and duly examined by this Assembly, *It is Voted and Resolved*, That the same be and hereby is allowed; and that *Eight Shillings and Fourpence* Lawful Money, being the Amount thereof, be paid the said *Anthony Low*, out of the General-Treasury.

A. Low allowed 8 s. 4 d.

An Account charged against the Colony by Mr. *Abraham Lockwood*, for Provisions by him supplied the Militia, when upon Duty at the Alarms on *Warwick* Neck, having been laid before and duly examined by this Assembly, *It is Voted and Resolved*, That the same

A. Lockwood allowed 7 s. 8 d.

be

be and hereby is allowed; and that *Seven Shillings and Eightpence* Lawful Money, being the Amount thereof, be paid the said *Abraham Lockwood*, out of the General-Treasury.

D. Austin allowed £6 per Annum for his House.
WHEREAS a small Dwelling-House belonging to *Daniel Austin*, situate at the Point in *Newport*, was removed to make Room for erecting the North Battery there; *It is therefore Voted and Resolved*, That *Six Pounds* Lawful Money be and is hereby allowed to be paid unto the said *Daniel Austin*, out of the General-Treasury, for each and every Year he shall be deprived of his House, to commence from the Time he was obliged to quit the same until it be restored unto him again, to enable him to hire a House.

Memorial of the Committee to act during the Recess of the Assembly, to Congress.
WHEREAS during the Recess of the General Assembly, such of the Members thereof as could conveniently be immediately convened did assemble, and thinking it to be expedient that *John Collins*, Esq; should present unto the Most Honorable the Continental Congress the following Memorial:

To the Most Honorable the Delegates of the United Colonies, in Congress, assembled at Philadelphia.

" IN the Absence of the Governor, and Deputy-Governor, Commodore *Esek Hopkins* hath applied to us for the Re-delivery of Twenty Pieces of Cannon, which he hath landed in this Colony: We have thought it absolutely necessary to detain them, until your Honors should be made acquainted with the Circumstances of the Colony, not doubting but that upon mature Consideration it would be thought best for the common Interest to permit them to remain here. We beg the most favourable Construction of this Measure, and assure your Honors, that no Persons living are more sensible of the Necessity of establishing the Authority of Congress, nor more ready to pay Obedience to it.

" YOUR Honors have doubtless frequently with Pain reflected upon the unhappy State of the Town of *Newport*, which was entirely defenceless, surrounded by a powerful

powerful naval Armament, and daily threatened with and in Danger of immediate Destruction; for it was inconteftibly in the Power of the *British* Fleet to destroy it at Pleasure. In this Situation it is not at all strange that near a third Part of the Inhabitants removed, and that a Majority of the Remainder were induced to temporize, and even to assume an Appearance rather unfriendly to the United Colonies. To this Situation alone is the former Conduct of *Newport* to be attributed, and not to Want of Spirit, or Love of their Country. In this State of Affairs the *British* Fleet quitted the Harbour, and Commodore *Hopkins* most providentially arrived with Twenty-six Cannon and some Shot, which he offered to the Town. The Inhabitants, elated with a Prospect of having this Means of Defence, assembled in a full Town-Meeting, and unanimously voted to work upon the necessary Fortifications, and to defend the Town, and immediately entered upon it with Vigour. This decisive Resolution gave every Friend to the United Colonies a new Spring, as many of us looked upon *Newport* as worse than lost to the common Cause. Three considerable Works have been erected: These Cannon have been with great Expedition mounted upon Carriages, and placed upon the Platforms, and the Town of *Newport* is now capable of being defended against all the Frigates in the *British* Navy. Fortifications are also making at *Bristol* Ferry, and on the East Side of *Rhode-Island*, which when compleated will effectually secure a Communication with the Continent, and enable us to defend that most valuable Island.

"We were happy in the Idea of having put a total Stop to supplying the Enemy, of destroying the very Seeds of Disaffection in the Colony, and of being an united People. We looked upon saving the Town of *Newport*, the commanding the Harbour, in which, from its Easiness of Access, Vessels from Sea may find a quick Protection under the Cannon of the Forts, and which will at all Times afford a safe Asylum to the Continental Ships, and to Privateers and their Prizes, as well as to other Vessels, and which, by Means of the Works now erected, may pass in and out in Spite of all the *British* Fleet, as Objects of very great Importance to the common Cause. But our pleasing Prospects are greatly interrupted by the Order to deliver Twenty of these Cannon to Messieurs *Hollingsworth* and *Richardson*, to be transported to *Philadelphia*. From the Face of it, which is directed to the Commodore, and in his Absence to Mr. *Tillinghast*, it appeared clearly to us that your Honors thought the Cannon were barely landed here, and had no Idea of their being fitted with Carriages, and planted in Forts erected purposely for their Reception.

" WE beg Leave to refer you for a general State of the Colony to the Memorial from the Assembly, which is now before your Honors, and is in no Degree exaggerated, by which you will be able to judge of the exposed Situation of the Colony, of its great Exertions for the common, as well as our own Defence, and of the utter Impossibility of our defending ourselves: To which we would add, that there are now in the Colony, exclusive of those brought by the Commodore, but Twenty-four Pieces of heavy Cannon, being Twenty-four and Eighteen Pounders.

" THE Assembly had contracted with the Owners of Furnace *Hope* for Sixty more, but the Commodore having brought Twenty-six heavy Cannon into the Colony, the Assembly consented that the Cannon for the Continental Ships should be first made, as the Owners of the Furnace could not possibly supply both Departments in Season, so that we have yet had but Four Eighteen Pounders from them; nor can the others be made under a long Time, unless a Stop be put to those making for the Ships.

" WE are informed by the Commodore that he landed Thirty-six heavy Cannon at *New-London*, which from its Situation can be defended with one Quarter of the Number required for the Defence of the Bay, Town, and Harbour of *Newport*. And when the Difference of the Towns of *Newport* and *New-London*,

in

June, 1776.

in Point of Number of Inhabitants and Value, in Point of Importance to the United Colonies, and in the Abilities of the two Colonies, of which they are a Part, to defend them, are confidered, we think it will not admit a Doubt from which Place the Twenty Cannon wanted are to be removed.

"We beg Leave alfo to mention to your Honors fome of the probable Confequences of depriving us of thofe Cannon. All the Difaffected, all the Lukewarm, and all the Timid, cry out that this Colony hath been totally neglected by Congrefs, while every other Colony that is expofed is defended by the Continental Troops, which the moft hearty in the common Caufe cannot deny; this, with the dangerous Situation of the Town of *Newport*, the Capital of the Colony, containing upwards of 1300 Dwelling-Houfes, and between 9 and 10,000 Souls, hath produced a very great Divifion, and was near overthrowing that Adminiftration which had fo greatly exerted the Force of the Colony. The Blow however was averted, and the moft feafonable Arrival of thofe Cannon, with the decifive Refolution of the Town of *Newport*, hath given Union, Spirit and Vigour to the Colony: Take them from us, and we cannot anfwer for the Event. The Town of *Newport* and the Ifland of *Rhode-Ifland* are loft. A fmall Part of that Army now at *Halifax*, may in their Way to the Weftward effect their Deftruction, without being detained three Days. It will be impoffible for the Inhabitants to defend themfelves: They will not even attempt it. There is Danger, that thofe People who are fo defirous of Reconciliation with *Great-Britain* upon any Terms, will gain the Afcendency, and of the Colony's being loft to *America*. Leave us the Cannon, we can fave *Newport*, which hath been induced in Confequence of their Arrival to take fuch Steps as muft bring upon them the *British* Arms, and who will be moft cruelly treated in being deprived of them. We can keep Poffeffion of *Rhode-Ifland*, which is of great Confequence to the Inhabitants and Trade of *Taunton* and *Swanfey* Rivers; and we fhall be a united People, ready with our Lives and Fortunes to fupport the Meafures of Congrefs.

"We

"We submit this Representation to your Honors, which will be delivered to you by *John Collins*, Esq; the First Assistant in this Colony, to whom we beg Leave to refer you for further Information, not in the least doubting that upon full Enquiry and Deliberation your Honors will consent that the Cannon remain here, until we can be otherwise supplied."

 Signed by Order and in Behalf of such Members of the General Assembly, as could conveniently be convened,

      By HENRY WARD, Sec'ry.

Providence, May 20, 1776.

WHEREUPON this Assembly taking the Premises into Consideration, *It is Voted and Resolved*, That the aforegoing Memorial be and the same is hereby approved.

Sheriff of Newport to take an Inventory of the Stock in E. Cole's Tan-Yard, &c.

IT is Voted and Resolved, That the Sheriff of the County of *Newport* immediately make an Inventory of the whole Stock in the Tan-Yard now in the Possession of Mr. *Edward Cole*, of *Newport*; and that the said Sheriff, with Col. *Christopher Lippet* and Mr. *Robert Taylor*, or the major Part of them, be a Committee to employ suitable Persons to work up the whole of the said Stock upon reasonable Terms, for the Benefit of the Colony.

IT is further Voted and Resolved, That Messieurs *Thomas Greene*, *Nathaniel Mumford*, and the aforesaid *Robert Taylor*, or the major Part of them, be and they are hereby appointed a Committee to examine and state the Accounts between the said *Edward Cole* and *George Rome*, respecting the said Tan-Yard, from the Time they entered into Partnership: That the said *Edward Cole* submit to the Inspection of the said Committee, under Oath, the original Contract of Partnership, and all Books of Accounts and Papers whatever relating to the said Tan-Yard, and to all Accounts of every Nature subsisting between them; and that the said Committee report to this Assembly as soon as may be.

           WHEREAS

June, 1776.

WHEREAS Meſſieurs *Nathaniel Mumford*, *Thomas Greene*, and *Gideon Mumford*, were appointed a Committee to enquire what Salt is now in the Colony belonging to the Government, and what the ſame coſt, including all Charges; and they having preſented unto this Aſſembly an Account, by them ſtated, with their Report thereon, as follow, *to wit :* — Coſt of the Salt belonging to Government aſcertained.

Dr. Salt, imported and purchaſed by the Colony of Rhode-Iſland.

1776. June.		£	s.	d.
To Amount of Cargo, Outfits and inward Charges, of Brig *Nancy*, fitted by *John Northup*,		310	13	6
To Amount of Cargo, Outfits and Loſs, of Sloop *Maryland*, by *Jacob Greene*,		445	14	10
To Amount of Cargo, Outfits and inward Charges, of Schooner *Abigail*, by *William Greene*,		317	14	4
To Amount of Cargo and Outfits of Brig ———, by *Smith* and *Mathewſon*,		216	16	5
To Amount of the Loſs of ſaid Brig,		480	0	0
To Amount of Cargo, Outfits and Portage-Bill, of the Schooner *Eagle*, by *Joſeph Stanton*, ſuppoſed,		303	0	0
To Amount of 1880 Buſhels purchaſed by *John Smith*, averaged as per *Paul Tew*'s Account, at 8 s.		752	0	0
To Amount of 617 Buſhels bought by *Sylveſter Child*, at 3 s.		92	11	0
Meaſuring and ſhifting Ditto,		0	18	0
To Amount of *Cory* and *Iriſh*'s Charges in fitting out two Veſſels to fetch Salt, ſtopt by Aſſembly,		172	13	0
By Salt imported in Brig *Nancy*,	2500 Buſhels.	£ 3091	19	1
Ditto in Schooner *Abigail*,	1880 Ditto.			
Ditto in Schooner *Eagle*,	1500 Ditto.			
Bought by *John Smith*,	1880 Ditto.			
Bought by *Sylveſter Child*,	617 Ditto.			
	8377 Buſhels.			

Allowed

June, 1776.

Allowed for Waftage, Wharfage and Storage, at $7\frac{1}{2}$ per Cent. } 628 Bufhels deducted.

Remain, 7749 at 7s. 11¾ £3091 19 1
At *Wefterly,* purchafed by Col. *Noyes,* } 130

7879 Bufhels.
Newport, June 13, 1776.

HAVING carefully examined the Accounts of the Cargoes, Outfits, and inward Charges, of the aforementioned Veffels, and the Loffes thereon fuftained, and averaged them with the Salt imported and purchafed, we find that it coft the Colony *Seven Shillings and Elevenpence Three Farthings per* Bufhel.

NATHANIEL MUMFORD,
THOMAS GREENE.

AND the Premifes being duly examined, *It is Voted and Refolved,* That the aforefaid Report be and hereby is accepted.

Committee to audit P. Tew's Account with the Colony.

IT *is Voted and Refolved,* That Col. *Amos Atwell,* Meffieurs *John Smith* and *John Brown,* be and they are hereby appointed a Committee to audit the Account of *Paul Tew,* Efq; with the Colony: And that they make Report to this Affembly.

Thanks of the Affembly to G. Wafhington, Efq;

IT *is Voted and Refolved,* That the Thanks of this Affembly be given to his Excellency *George Wafhington,* Efq; Commander in Chief of the Forces of the United Colonies, for his favourable Reprefentation of the State of this Colony to the Moft Honorable the Continental Congrefs, and Interpofition in procuring the Colony's Brigade to be taken into Continental Pay: And that his Honor the Governor be requefted to tranfmit to his Excellency a Copy of this Vote.

Committee to prepare a Bill for eftablifh-

IT *is Voted and Refolved,* That *Jonathan Arnold, Henry Marchant,* and *Henry Ward,* Efquires, be and they

June, 1776.   85

they are hereby appointed a Committee to prepare a Bill for establishing suitable Offices at *Newport* and *Providence*, for entering and clearing Vessels, and fixing the Fees of the Officers. *{ing Offices at Newport and Providence, for entering Vessels, &c.}*

WHEREAS Capt. *Matthew Allen*, of *Barrington*, preferred his Petition to this Assembly, setting forth, That he had the Command of a Company in Col. *Church's* Regiment, the last Summer's Campaign: That in making out a Return of his Company to the Colonel, in order that his said Company should receive their Wages, he inadvertently omitted to return three of the Soldiers Names belonging thereto: That their Wages amount to *Six Pounds* Lawful Money, which they were entitled to receive, and were not paid by the said Colonel: That the Petitioner paid the said Sum to them, out of his own Monies; and thereupon besought this Assembly that the same might be allowed and paid him, out of the General-Treasury: Whereupon this Assembly taking the Premises into Consideration, and having duly examined the same, *Do Vote and Resolve*, That the Prayer of said Petition be and hereby is granted; and that the aforesaid Sum of *Six Pounds* be paid unto the said *Matthew Allen*, out of the General-Treasury. *{M. Allen granted £6.}*

WHEREAS the Inhabitants of the Town of *Newport*, in Town-Meeting legally assembled, on the Twenty-ninth Day of *April* last, unanimously Voted, That they would defend the said Town, and ordered that the Inhabitants should work upon the Fortifications, upon the Penalty of paying *Three Shillings* per Day, for each and every Day's Neglect; and at a Meeting held on the Twenty fifth Day of *May* last, ordered, that the Fines of the Delinquents should be collected by *William Davis*; and that in case of Refusal he should destrain: And whereas some Doubts have arisen respecting the Authority of the said Town Meetings to pass the said Votes: *{Power of the Towns to make bye-laws ascertained.}*

IT is therefore *Resolved* and *Declared*, and it is hereby *Declared* by this *Assembly*, That by the Acts of Incorporation

corporation of the several Towns in this Colony, they are and ever were sufficiently authorized and empowered to make and ordain Acts, Laws, Orders and Regulations, binding upon their respective Inhabitants, in all Cases whatever, for their Advantage, Safety and Defence, and to impose such Fines and Penalties for the Breaches thereof, as they shall deem meet, and to appoint a Person or Persons to collect such Fines and Penalties, with Power to distrain, in case of Refusal or Neglect to pay the same; provided such Acts, Laws, Orders and Regulations, are not repugnant to the Acts, Laws, Orders and Regulations, of this General Assembly.

S. Johnson allowed £50 10s.

WHEREAS Mr. *Samuel Johnson* exhibited unto this Assembly an Account, by him charged against the Colony, for Four Pieces of Cannon, for the Use of the Colony: And the said Account being duly examined, *It is Voted and Resolved*, That the same be and hereby is allowed; and that *Fifty Pounds and Ten Shillings*, being the Amount of said Account, be paid unto the said *Samuel Johnson*, out of the General-Treasury.

J. Lippet allowed £1 9s. 9d.

WHEREAS Mr. *Joseph Lippet* exhibited unto this Assembly an Account, by him charged, for victualling Part of Capt. *Reuben Whitman*'s Company of Militia, at the Alarm upon *Warwick* Neck: Which said Account being duly examined, *It is Voted and Resolved*, That the same be and hereby is allowed; and that *One Pound Nine Shillings and Ninepence*, being the Amount thereof, be paid unto the said *Joseph Lippet*, out of the General-Treasury.

J. Clark allowed £90

WHEREAS Mr. *Jeremiah Clarke* exhibited unto this Assembly an Account, by him charged for Six Pieces of Cannon delivered Brigadier-General *West*, for the Use of the Colony: Which said Account being duly examined, *It is Voted and Resolved*, That the same be and hereby is allowed; and that *Ninety Pounds* Lawful Money, being the Amount thereof, be paid unto the said *Jeremiah Clarke*, out of the General-Treasury.

WHEREAS

June, 1776.

WHEREAS Mr. *Daniel Chace* exhibited unto this Assembly an Account, by him charged for the Use of a Feather-Bed, made Use of for a wounded Prisoner taken at *Prudence,* which was damaged: Which said Account being duly examined, *It is Voted and Resolved,* That *One Pound Five Shillings* Lawful Money, for the said Damage, be paid unto the said *Daniel Chace,* out of the General-Treasury.

D. Chace allowed £1 5s.

WHEREAS Messieurs *William Barton, William Stevens, Nathaniel Jacobs,* jun. and *Samuel Chace,* exhibited unto this Assembly an Account, by them charged for their Time, Expence, and Horse-hire, in going to *Boston,* and bringing Ten Prisoners to *Providence:* Which said Account being duly examined, *It is Voted and Resolved,* That the same be and hereby is allowed; and that the Amount thereof, being *Thirteen Pounds Eight Shillings and Sevenpence* Lawful Money, be paid unto the said *William Barton, William Stevens, Nathaniel Jacobs,* jun. and *Samuel Chace,* out of the General-Treasury.

W. Barton, W. Stevens, N. Jacobs, jun. and S. Chace, allowed £13 8s. 7d.

IT is *Voted and Resolved,* That the Persons appointed by this Assembly to take Possession of Estates belonging to Persons disaffected to the United Colonies, in Behalf of and for the Use of the Government, be and they are hereby directed immediately to render an Account, in Writing, of their Proceedings therein to this Assembly.

Persons appointed to take Possession of the Estates of disaffected Persons, to render an Account thereof.

WHEREAS *William Potter* and *John Northup,* Esquires, who were appointed at the last Session a Committee to let out, in Behalf of the Colony, all the real Estates in the County of *King's County,* lately belonging to Persons disaffected to the United Colonies, and heretofore ordered by this Assembly to be taken into Possession by the Sheriff of said County, &c. did upon a Copy of their Appointment make Report; to which they subjoined an Account, by them charged against the Colony, as follows, *to wit*:

Report of the Committee appointed to lease Estates taken into Possession of the Colony.

WE the Subscribers, with *Peter Phillips,* Esq; in Obedience to the within Order, have leased all the Estates

taken

taken into Possession by the Sheriff of the County of *King's County*, as within mentioned, *to wit* : The Estate lately belonging to the Heirs of *John Borland*, consisting of two Tracts of Land, one of which we have let to *Rowland Robinson*, Esq; and the other to Mr. *Christopher Robinson* : The Estate lately belonging to Dr. *Thomas Moffatt*, we have let to Mr. *Charles Dyre:* The Estate lately belonging to *George Rome*, we have let to Mr. *Stephen Boyer* ; and the Estate lately belonging to *Samuel Sewal*, consisting of two Tracts, one of which we have leased to Mr. *Silas Niles*, and the other to Mr. *David Austin* ; and have taken written Leases thereof, which we herewith present to your Honors. We have also disposed of, at public Vendue, Four Horses lately belonging to the said *George Rome*, for the Sum of *Forty-nine Pounds Sixteen Shillings* ; which we are ready to account for.

WILLIAM POTTER,
JOHN NORTHUP.

The Colony to the said Committee, Dr.

	£	s	d
To *William Potter*, for his Service in performing the above mentioned Business, 7 Days, at 6 s. per Day,	2	2	0
To *Peter Phillips*, for the same, 6 Days,	1	16	0
For advertising the Stock,	0	5	0
	2	1	0
To *John Northup*, for his Service as above, 8 Days,	2	8	0
For Cash paid the Vendue-Master,	1	4	11
For Ditto paid *J. Coggeshall*, for drawing the Writings,	0	10	0
	4	2	11
	£8	5	11

Committee allowed £8 5s. 11d.

BOTH which being duly considered, *It is Voted and Resolved*, That the said Report be accepted ; that the said Account of the Committee be allowed, and paid out of the General-Treasury, in the aforesaid Proportions ; and that the Committee pay the said Sum of

Forty-

June, 1776. 89

Forty-nine *Pounds Sixteen Shillings* into the General-Treasury.

IT is *Voted and Resolved,* That Messieurs *Nathaniel Mumford, Thomas Greene,* and *Gideon Mumford,* be and they, or the major Part of them, are hereby appointed a Committee to prepare a State of the Demands of this Colony upon the Continental Treasury; and that they lay the same before this Assembly at the next Session, in order that it may be transmitted with the Vouchers to the Treasury-Office. Committee to state the Demands of the Colony upon the Continental Treasury.

IT is *Voted and Resolved,* That all the Arrearages of Rents due from the Tenants in Possession of the Lands lately belonging to Persons disaffected to the *American* Cause, and taken into Possession of this Colony, be paid into the General-Treasury: That Col. *John Cooke,* for the County of *Newport;* Paul *Tew,* Esq; for the County of *Providence*; *William Potter,* Esq; for the County of *King's County*; and Mr. *Cromel Child,* for the County of *Bristol,* be and they are hereby appointed a Committee to enquire into and settle said Arrearages: That the Secretary deliver to the General-Treasurer all the Leases and Papers relating to said Estates that are in his Possession: And that in case the said Arrearages be not paid within Two Months after the Rising of this Assembly, the General-Treasurer be and he is hereby directed to sue for the same. Resolve relating to Estates taken into Possession by the Colony.

WHEREAS Mr. *Benjamin Shearman* exhibited unto this Assembly an Account, by him charged against the Colony, for the Use of his Boat seven Months, which was taken for the Service of the Colony, by General *Hopkins:* It is *Voted and Resolved,* upon due Examination, That the same be allowed; and that *Two Pounds Sixteen Shillings* Lawful Money, being the Amount thereof, be paid the said *Benjamin Shearman,* out of the General-Treasury. B. Shearman allowed £ 2 16 s.

WHEREAS at the last Session *Nedebiah Wilkinson* was by Mistake chosen First Lieutenant, and *Edward Thompson* Second Lieutenant, of the Independent Company, called

June, 1776.

Mistake in the Choice of Officers of the Smithfield and Cumberland Rangers rectified.

called the *Smithfield* and *Cumberland* Rangers, when it was the Intention of the said Company that the said *Edward Thompson* should have been the First, and the said *Nedebiah Wilkinson* the Second Lieutenant: *It is therefore Voted and Resolved,* That the said Choice be and the same is hereby made null; that the said *Edward Thompson* be and he is hereby appointed First Lieutenant, and the said *Nedebiah Wilkinson* Second Lieutenant, of the said Company; and that they be commissioned accordingly.

S. Southwick allowed £6 6s. 2d.

Whereas Mr. *Solomon Southwick* exhibited unto this Assembly an Account, amounting to *Thirteen Pounds Sixteen Shillings and Twopence,* by him charged against the Colony, for Paper supplied the Secretary for the Use of the Colony, for printing the Rules and Regulations of the Army, for inserting divers Acts of Assembly, and Advertisements, in the *Newport* Mercury, *&c.* and deducted therefrom *Seven Pounds Ten Shillings,* for the nett Amount of the Post-Office, while the same was under the Direction of the Colony: *It is Voted and Resolved,* upon due Examination of the said Account, That the same be and hereby is allowed; and that *Six Pounds Six Shillings and Twopence,* being the Balance thereof, be paid the said *Solomon Southwick,* out of the General-Treasury.

J. Frost's Estate sequestered.

IT is Voted and Resolved, That the Sheriff of the County of *Newport* be and he is hereby directed to take Possession, in Behalf of the Colony, of a Dwelling-House and Lot, situate in *Newport,* in the said County, belonging to *James Frost,* who hath engaged in the Service of the Enemies to the United Colonies: But that the Wife of the said *James Frost* may reside on the Premises, or receive the Rents and Profits thereof, until further Orders from this Assembly.

Sheriff of the County of Newport to take E. Cole into Custody.

Whereas the Committee appointed to examine and state the Accounts between *George Rome* and *Edward Cole,* have informed this Assembly, that the said *Edward Cole* refuseth to submit, under Oath, the Accounts, Papers, *&c.* to the Inspection of the said Committee:

It

It is therefore Voted and Resolved, That the said *Edward Cole* be immediately taken into Custody by the Sheriff of the County of *Newport*, and safely kept until he shall submit the said Accounts, &c. to the Inspection of the said Committee, agreeable to the Act of this Assembly made in that Behalf.

IN Council was read the Return of the Officers chosen for the Independent Company, called the *Kentish Guards*, who are as follow: [Officers of the *Kentish Guards*.]

Richard Fry, Captain,
Hopkins Cooke, First Lieutenant,
Thomas Holden, Second Lieutenant,
Sylvester Greene, Ensign.

AND the same being duly considered, *It is Voted*, That the said Choice be and hereby is approved.

IT is Voted and Resolved, That *William Potter*, Esq; be and he is hereby directed to procure the Court-House in *South-Kingstown* to be glazed, painted and finished, as soon as possible; and that he be empowered to draw *Three Hundred Pounds* Lawful Money out of the General-Treasury, for that Purpose. [Court-House in *King's* County to be finished.]

WHEREAS Mr. *John Smith* exhibited unto this Assembly an Account, by him charged against the Colony, for two Reams of Paper, delivered the Secretary, for the Use of the Colony: *It is Voted and Resolved*, upon due Examination, That the said Account be and the same is hereby allowed; and that *Three Pounds* Lawful Money, being the Amount thereof, be paid the said *John Smith*, out of the General-Treasury. [*J. Smith* allowed £ 3.]

IT is Voted and Resolved, That all the Soldiers who were stationed at *Block-Island*, be paid the Wages still due to them, by *John Northup*, and *Joseph Stanton*, jun. Esquires, two of the Committee of Safety, as soon as conveniently may be; and that they make Report to this Assembly at the next Session. [Soldiers at *Block-Island* to be paid.]

IN Council was read the Return of the Officers chosen for the Company called the *North-Providence Rangers*, who are as follow: [Officers for the *North-Providence Rangers*.]

K *John*

John Angell (Son of *Stephen*) Captain,
Thomas Olney, jun. Lieutenant,
Joseph Hawkins, jun. Ensign.

AND the same being duly considered, *It is Voted and Resolved*, That the said Choice be and hereby is approved.

※※※※※※※※※

An ACT permitting Inoculation for the Small-Pox in this Colony.

Act permitting Inoculation.

WHEREAS the Small-Pox hath made the most dreadful Ravages in the Army lately before *Quebec*, which was a principal Cause of raising the Blockade of that City, and there is great Danger that the Inhabitants of the United Colonies may, by the Prevalence of that dreadful Distemper, be rendered incapable of Defence at a Time when their Safety may depend upon their most vigorous Exertions: And whereas that Distemper taken by Inoculation is so easy and light, and the Method of Treatment so beneficial, that any Number of Persons inoculated are more likely to live, than the same Number of Persons not inoculated; and as by introducing the Practice of Inoculation with Prudence and Caution, the greater Part of the male Inhabitants of the Colonies may soon get over that terrible Disease, and the fatal Consequences to be apprehended from our Armies being infected therewith be averted:

BE it therefore Enacted by this General Assembly, and by the Authority thereof it is Enacted, That one Hospital may be established for inoculating for the Small-Pox in each County in this Colony, in such Town as the Majority of the Deputies in the County, in a Meeting duly warned, shall agree upon: That the Hospital in the Town which shall be so agreed upon shall be fixed in some suitable and retired Place in such Town, under the Direction of the Town-Council, or of such Committee as the Town shall appoint: Provided that when such Hospital shall be improved for that Purpose, the Town shall

shall mark off the Ground round said Hospital, at a Distance not less than Two Hundred Yards every Way therefrom, and set and maintain a sufficient Guard, to prevent all Persons in the Hospital from going beyond those Limits, and all Persons without, from passing within One Hundred Yards of them, without the Permission of the Directors of the Hospital, upon the Penalty of forfeiting and paying as a Fine, into the General-Treasury, *One Hundred Pounds* Lawful Money, to be recovered of the Town-Treasurer of such Town, by the General-Treasurer, at any Inferior Court of Common Pleas in the Colony.

A N D be it further Enacted by the Authority aforesaid, That every Person passing the said Limits, without Permission as aforesaid, shall forfeit and pay as a Fine *Fifteen Pounds* Lawful Money, to and for the Use of such Town, to be recovered by the Town-Treasurer, at a special Court, to be called and holden in the same Manner as special Courts are called and held in other Cases; and shall also suffer Three Months Imprisonment, without Bail or Mainprize.

A N D be it further Enacted by the Authority aforesaid, That it shall be the Duty of the said Guard, and they are hereby empowered, to apprehend and immediately commit to Gaol every Person who shall transgress with respect to the said Limits, there to remain until he shall be acquitted, or the Sentence passed upon him be executed; unless such Transgressor shall be under Inoculation, in which case he shall be carefully kept within the said Limits until he shall be recovered and cleansed, and then be committed to Gaol as aforesaid.

A N D it is further Enacted, That if any Person, being so inoculated, shall after his Recovery from the Small-Pox go beyond the said Limits, without a Certificate of his being thoroughly cleansed therefrom, together with the wearing Apparel he shall carry out with him, he shall, in Default thereof, be liable to the Penalty of *Thirty Pounds* Lawful Money, to be recovered in Manner as above directed. And if any Person having such Certificate, shall by himself, or by Means of the Apparel he may carry out with him, communicate the

Small-

Small-Pox to any Person without the Hospital, the Doctor or Physician of such Hospital shall be liable to the Penalty of *Thirty Pounds* Lawful Money, to be recovered in Manner as above directed.

A N D be it further Enacted by the Authority aforesaid, That no Person shall carry out from the Hospital, where he may be inoculated, any Bedding or other Articles, Linen Sheets and his wearing Apparel as aforesaid excepted; and that every Article which he shall carry out shall be particularly enumerated in the Certificate from the Doctor or Physician of such Hospital, under the Penalty of *Thirty Pounds* Lawful Money, to be recovered of such inoculated Person so offending in Manner as above directed.

A N D be it further Enacted by the Authority aforesaid, That any Town in which an Hospital shall be established as aforesaid, be and hereby is empowered to make such further Regulations, to prevent communicating the Infection from the Hospital in such Town, and to lay such Fines and Penalties upon the Offenders as they shall think proper : And that all Acts made by such Town in that Behalf shall be of the same Force and Validity as if enacted by this General Assembly.

※※※※※※※※※※※※

Protest against the Act permitting Inoculation.

THE Subscribers protest against this Bill's passing into an Act, for the following Reasons, *to wit :*

FIRST, For that although we urged, that in a case of such vast Importance as intimately affects the Lives, Safety, and Well-being of the Community, the Consent and Approbation of our respective Constituents ought to have been first had and obtained, yet this Motion hath been rejected.

SECONDLY, For that an Act of this Kind hath not been suffered to continue but for a short Time in any of the *New-England* Colonies ; and that where it hath been permitted or winked at, it is now entirely discontinued, and discountenanced.

THIRDLY,

THIRDLY, For that there is in this Act no Provision made for the Poor, who are by far the much more numerous Part of the Community.

JOHN G. WANTON, BENJAMIN UNDERWOOD,
JOSHUA BABCOCK, THOMAS WELLS,
JOHN NORTHUP, SYLVESTER GARDNER,
JOSHUA BARKER, EDWARD SANDS, jun.
THOMAS FREEBODY, JOHN THURSTON.

IT is *Voted and Resolved*, That Mr. *John Waterman* be and he is hereby appointed and empowered to agree with some suitable Person, upon the best Terms he can, to work in the Powder-Mill belonging to the Colony. *J. Waterman to employ a Person in the Colony's Powder-Mill.*

IT is *Voted and Resolved*, That his Honor the Deputy-Governor, *William Potter, George Sears, Jonathan Arnold, William Greene* and *Henry Ward*, Esquires, be and they are hereby appointed a Committee to enquire into the Circumstances of the Uneasiness, subsisting among a Number of the Officers of the Colony's Brigade, stationed upon *Rhode-Island*, respecting Major *Barton*; and that they make Report to this Assembly as soon as may be. *Committee to enquire into the Uneasiness in the Brigade respecting Major Barton.*

IN Pursuance of the Recommendation of the Most Honorable the Continental Congress, *Resolved,* That an Account be immediately taken of the Number of the Inhabitants in each Town in this Colony: That the Persons whose Names are set down in the subsequent List be and they are hereby appointed a Committee for that Purpose, *to wit:* *Account to be taken of the Number of Inhabitants in the Colony.*

Newport. Messieurs *George Sears, William Coddington,* and *Gideon Wanton.*
Providence. Messieurs *Martin Seamans* and *Theodore Foster.*
Portsmouth. Mr. *John Coddington.*
Warwick. Mr. *Charles Holden.*
Westerly. Messieurs *Ichabod Babcock* and *Joseph Crandall.*
New-Shoreham. Mr. *Edward Sands,* jun.

North-Kingstown. Mr. *Joseph Coggeshall.*
South-Kingstown. Mr. *Daniel Rodman.*
East-Greenwich. Mr. *Thomas Sheffield.*
Jamestown. Mr. *Benjamin Underwood.*
Smithfield. Mr. *Daniel Mowry,* jun.
Scituate. Mr. *Christopher Potter,* or Mr. *William West.*
Gloucester. Mr. *Zebedee Hopkins,* jun.
Charlestown. Mr. *Jonathan Hazard.*
West-Greenwich. Mr. *Judiah Aylsworth.*
Coventry. Mr. *Ephraim Westcot.*
Exeter. Mr. *George Pierce.*
Middletown. Mr. *John Barker.*
Bristol. Mr. *Shearjashub Bourn.*
Tiverton. Messieurs *John Cooke* and *Walter Cooke.*
Little-Compton. Mr. *Thomas Brownell.*
Warren. Mr. *William Miller.*
Cumberland. Mr. *John Dexter.*
Richmond. Mr. *Richard Bailey.*
Cranston. Mr. *Zuriel Waterman.*
Hopkinton. Mr. *Thomas Wells.*
Johnston. Mr. *John Fenner.*
North-Providence. Mr. *Jonathan Jenckes,* jun. And,
Barrington. Mr. *Thomas Allen.*

THAT they take the Account in the same Manner as the Inhabitants of this Colony were last numbered: That they be under Engagement for the faithful Discharge of the Trust reposed in them, and that they make Report to this Assembly at the next Session.

Act restraining the Inhabitants of *New-Shoreham.*

THIS Assembly deploring the unhappy Situation of the Inhabitants of *New-Shoreham,* and willing to give them every Relief in their Power; and being also necessitated to provide for the general Safety, *Do Resolve,* in Addition to and Amendment of the Act passed at the last Session respecting the said Island, That the Committee appointed in the said Act may permit such of the Inhabitants of the said Island as they can confide in, to go to *Pawcatuck* River, to procure at the Mills there such a Quantity of Meal as shall be necessary for the Inhabitants of the said Island;
they

they taking the fame and other Neceffaries on board under the Direction and with the written Permiffion of *George Sheffield* and *Phinehas Clarke*, or either of them, who are hereby directed to tranfmit to the faid Committee an Account of all the Articles fo taken on board for the faid Ifland: That the faid Committee be empowered to permit fuch Inhabitants of the faid Ifland as they can confide in, to proceed to any Part of the Colony, to tranfact the neceffary Bufinefs of the Ifland; and that no other Perfon belonging to the faid Ifland, befides the Deputies, fhall go to any other Part of the Colony, excepting to *Goat-Ifland*, in the Townfhip of *Newport*, upon the Penalty of being committed to Gaol, as in the aforefaid Act is directed.

James Honeyman, Efq; Advocate-General of the Court of Vice-Admiralty in this Colony, under the Crown of *Great-Britain*, having appeared before and informed this Affembly, that if his holding the faid Office be difagreeable to the Colony, he will deliver up his Commiffion: It is Voted and Refolved, That his holding the fame is difagreeable to the Colony; and that the Sheriff of the County of *Newport* call upon the faid *James Honeyman* to receive the faid Commiffion, and that he deliver it to his Honor the Governor, to be lodged in the Secretary's Office.

J. Honeyman to deliver up his Commiffion as Advocate-General of the Court of Vice-Admiralty.

WHEREAS *John Jepfon*, Efq; and Mr. *Jofhua Barker*, who were at the laft Seffion appointed a Committee to divide the Line of Fence between the Lands of *Thomas Coggefhall*, of *Middletown*, and the Eftate lately belonging to *George Rome*, lying in faid Town, taken into Poffeffion of the Colony, and to determine what Part of the faid Fence fhall be maintained by the Colony, &c. having performed the faid Bufinefs, prefented unto this Affembly their Report, which is as follows, *to wit*:

Report of the Committee appointed to fettle the Maintenance of the Fence between T. Coggefhall's Farm, and that lately belonging to G. Rome.

MEMORANDUM of a Divifion in the Line of Fence between the Farm of *Thomas Coggefhall*, and a certain Piece of Meadow Land that *George Rome* purchafed of *Gideon Coggefhall*, and is now in Poffeffion of *William Wilbur*,

Wilbur, under the Government, *that is to say:* The said *Thomas Coggeshall* shall maintain Twenty-seven Rods, beginning at the Road, and extending Southward to a certain Mark in the Wall; and the said *William Wilbur*, or the Government, shall maintain the Remainder, which is Thirty-five Rods, and extends to Land of *William Stoddard*, now in the Possession of *Thomas Weaver* (Son of *Clement*.) Divided this 25th Day of *May*, *A. D.* 1776, according to an Act of Government, by us,

JOHN JEPSON,
JOSHUA BARKER.

MEMORANDUM of a Division in the Line of Fence between the Farm formerly belonging to *George Rome*, and now in the Possession of *William Wilbur*, under the Government, and the Farm of *Thomas Coggeshall*, that is to say: The said *Thomas Coggeshall* shall maintain Seventy-five Rods, beginning at the Head of *Jonathan Coggeshall*'s Meadow, and extending Westward to a certain Mark in the Wall; and the said *William Wilbur*, or the Government, shall maintain Seventy-five Rods, beginning at the above mentioned Mark in the Wall, and extending Westward as far as high Water Mark; and the Water-Fence shall be maintained equally between both Parties. Divided this 25th Day of *May*, *A. D.* 1776, by us, according to an Act of Government.

JOHN JEPSON,
JOSHUA BARKER.

AND the Premises being duly considered, *It is Voted and Resolved*, That the said Report be and the same is hereby accepted.

Allowance to *J. Coon*, for taking Care of *A. Coon*, a Soldier.

WHEREAS Capt. *John Coon*, of *Hopkinton*, represented unto this Assembly, that at the Request of Capt. *Ethan Clarke* he took into his Care *Arnold Coon*, a sick Soldier, in the said *Ethan Clarke*'s Company, and provided him with Physicians, Nurses, *&c.* until he died; and prayed this Assembly to make him an Allowance therefor: *It is Voted and Resolved*, upon due

due Confideration of the Matter, That there be allowed and paid, out of the General-Treafury, to the faid *John Coon*, the fame monthly Wages as are allowed to Soldiers in the Service of this Colony, from the Time the faid *Arnold Coon* was taken fick, unto the laft Day of *December* laft.

IT is *Voted and Refolved*, That all the Salt belonging to the Colony be divided among the feveral Towns, in Proportion to the Number of Polls in each Town, which is to be afcertained by the Account of the Number of Inhabitants in the Colony, at this Seffion ordered to be taken; that the fame be delivered by Meffieurs *John Smith, William Greene, John Northup, Jofeph Stanton*, jun. and *Sylvefter Child*; that each Town be at the Coft of tranfporting its Proportion; and that it be difpofed of at the Difcretion of each Town, at the Rate of *Six Shillings per* Bufhel, for Cafh only, by fuch Perfons as the Town fhall appoint.

The Colony's Salt proportioned to the feveral Towns.

AND it is further *Voted and Refolved*, That each Town may immediately receive the following Quantity, in Part of its faid Proportion, *to wit*:

Newport,	200 Bufhels.
Providence,	100
Portfmouth,	50
Warwick,	100
Wefterly,	100
New-Shoreham,	30
North-Kingftown,	100
South-Kingftown,	150
Eaft-Greenwich,	100
Jameftown,	30
Smithfield,	150
Scituate,	150
Gloucefter,	120
Charleftown,	60
Weft-Greenwich,	80
Coventry,	80
Exeter,	50
Middletown,	40
Briftol,	50
Tiverton,	60

Little-Compton,	50 Bushels.
Warren,	50
Cumberland,	60
Richmond,	50
Cranston,	100
Hopkinton,	80
Johnston,	50
North-Providence,	20
Barrington,	25

J. Jepson and J. Barker allowed £ 1 4s.

WHEREAS *John Jepson*, Esq; and Mr. *Joshua Barker*, exhibited unto this Assembly an Account, by them charged against the Colony, for their Service in running two dividing Lines of Fence, between the Land lately belonging to *George Rome*, and the Land of *Thomas Coggeshall*; and for having their Report recorded: *It is Voted and Resolved*, upon due Examination of the said Account, That the same be and hereby is allowed; and that *One Pound Four Shillings* Lawful Money, being the Amount thereof, be paid the said *John Jepson* and *Joshua Barker*, out of the General-Treasury.

Petition of J. Cagwine and others referred to the Committee of Safety.

WHEREAS *James Cagwine*, *Benjamin Daly*, and *Daniel Eldred*, by Petition represented unto this Assembly, that they were Soldiers in Capt. *Christopher Smith*'s Company, in the Service of this Colony, and served upon *Block-Island*, under Lieut. *Sweet*; and that they have not been paid the whole of their Wages, and prayed this Assembly to order Payment of the Wages still due to them: *It is therefore Voted and Resolved*, That the Committee of Safety, for the County of *Kent*, make Enquiry into the Truth of the Matters set forth in the said Petition, and pay the above named *James Cagwine*, *Benjamin Daley*, and *Daniel Eldred*, the Sums that shall appear to be due to them; making Report to this Assembly before Payment.

J. Coddington allowed £ 6.

WHEREAS Mr. *John Coddington* exhibited unto this Assembly an Account, by him charged against the Colony, for a Cedar Boat, by him supplied for the Service of the Colony: *It is Voted and Resolved*, upon

due

June, 1776.

due Confideration of the faid Account, That *Six Pounds* thereof, and no more, be allowed and paid the faid *John Coddington,* out of the General-Treafury.

WHEREAS Mr. *John Goddard* exhibited unto this Affembly fix feveral Accounts, by him charged againft the Colony, for the Tranfportation by Water of feveral Detachments of the Colony's Brigade, from and to different Places at divers Times, and the Ufe made of and Damage done to his Boat by the faid Brigade: *It is Voted and Refolved,* upon due Examination, That *Four Pounds Thirteen Shillings and Eightpence Halfpenny* be allowed and paid the faid *John Goddard,* out of the General-Treafury; which fhall be in full Satisfaction for the faid fix Accounts.

J. Goddard allowed £4 13*s.* 8*d.*½

WHEREAS Mr. *Nathaniel Waldron* exhibited unto this Affembly an Account, by him charged againft the Colony, for billeting a Company of Soldiers belonging to the Colony's Brigade, *&c. It is Voted and Refolved,* upon due Examination of the faid Account, That the fame be and hereby is allowed; and that *One Pound Nineteen Shillings and Tenpence* Lawful Money, being the Amount thereof, be paid the faid *Nathaniel Waldron,* out of the General-Treafury.

N. Waldron allowed £1 19*s.* 10*d.*

WHEREAS Mr. *Jonathan Peck* exhibited unto this Affembly an Account, by him charged againft the Colony, for Plank furnifhed by him for the Platforms in the Fort at *Briftol* Ferry: *It is Voted and Refolved,* upon due Examination, That the faid Account be allowed; and that *One Pound Twelve Shillings,* being the Amount thereof, be paid the faid *Jonathan Peck,* out of the General-Treafury.

J. Peck allowed £1 12*s.*

WHEREAS Mr. *James Smith* exhibited unto this Affembly an Account, by him charged againft the Colony, for Timber fupplied by him for the Platforms in the Fort at *Briftol* Ferry: *It is Voted and Refolved,* upon due Examination of the faid Account, That the fame be and hereby is allowed; and that *Two Pounds Four Shillings and Fourpence Halfpenny* Lawful

J. Smith allowed £2 4*s.* 4*d.*½

Lawful Money, being the Amount thereof, be paid the said *James Smith*, out of the General-Treasury.

J. Weſt allowed 7 s.

WHEREAS Mr. *John Weſt* exhibited unto this Aſſembly an Account, by him charged againſt the Colony, for Plank by him provided for the Platforms in the Fort at *Briſtol* Ferry, and carting the ſame : *It is Voted and Reſolved*, upon due Examination thereof, That the ſame be and hereby is allowed ; and that *Seven Shillings*, being the Amount thereof, be paid the ſaid *John Weſt*, out of the General-Treaſury.

S. Smith allowed £ 1 12 s. 8 d. ¼

WHEREAS Mr. *Stephen Smith* exhibited unto this Aſſembly an Account, by him charged againſt the Colony, for Plank and Timber by him provided for the Platforms in the Fort at *Briſtol* Ferry : *It is Voted and Reſolved*, upon due Examination of the ſaid Account, That the ſame be and hereby is allowed ; and that *One Pound Twelve Shillings and Eightpence One Farthing* Lawful Money, being the Amount thereof, be paid the ſaid *Stephen Smith*, out of the General-Treaſury.

P. Tew allowed £ 22 1 s. 9 d.

WHEREAS *Paul Tew*, Eſq; Sheriff of the County of *Providence*, exhibited unto this Aſſembly an Account, by him charged againſt the Colony, for Attendance upon the General Aſſembly, and the Superior and Inferior Courts in the County aforeſaid, for Wood provided for the Court-Houſe, for Caſh paid by him for cleaning and ſanding the ſaid Court-Houſe, *&c. It is Voted and Reſolved*, upon due Examination, That *Twenty-two Pounds One Shilling and Ninepence* Lawful Money be allowed, and paid to the ſaid *Paul Tew*, out of the General-Treaſury, which ſhall be in full Satisfaction for the ſame.

C. Child allowed £ 27 2

WHEREAS Mr. *Cromel Child* exhibited unto this Aſſembly an Account, by him charged againſt the Colony, for making Twenty-one Carriages for Cannon, for the Colony, and his Time and Expences in going to *Providence*, to ſend the Cannon to *Warren*:

It

It is Voted and Resolved, upon due Examination thereof, That the said Account be and hereby is allowed; and that *Two Hundred and Seventeen Pounds Two Shillings* Lawful Money, being the Amount of the same, be paid the said *Cromel Child*, out of the General-Treasury.

WHEREAS *James Arnold*, jun. Esq; exhibited unto this Assembly an Account, by him charged against the Colony, for Materials provided for and laying a Platform in the Battery upon *Long-Neck*, in *Cranston*, for building a Watch-House there, and for making Field-Carriages for two Eighteen Pounders, and one other Cannon: *It is Voted and Resolved*, upon due Examination of the said Account, That the same be and hereby is allowed; and that *Seventy-five Pounds Sixteen Shillings and Twopence* Lawful Money, being the Balance due thereon, be paid the said *James Arnold*, jun. out of the General-Treasury.

J. Arnold, jun. allowed £ 75 16 s. 2 d.

WHEREAS Mr. *John Mumford* exhibited unto this Assembly an Account, by him charged against the Colony, for Provisions for Capt. *Barton*'s Company, in the Regiment under the Command of Col. *Richmond*; and for the Hire of his Horse divers Times for the Use of the said Company: *It is Voted and Resolved*, upon due Examination of the said Account, That *Two Pounds Sixteen Shillings and Tenpence* Lawful Money be allowed and paid the said *John Mumford*, out of the General-Treasury; which shall be in full Satisfaction for the same.

J. Mumford allowed £ 2 16 s. 10 d.

WHEREAS Mr. *Caleb Carr* exhibited unto this Assembly an Account, by him charged against the Colony, for Wood and Provisions supplied Capt. *Throop*'s Company, in Col. *Richmond*'s Regiment: *It is Voted and Resolved*, upon due Examination of the said Account, That the same be and hereby is allowed; and that *Four Pounds Five Shillings and Sixpence* Lawful Money, being the Amount thereof, be paid the said *Caleb Carr*, out of the General-Treasury.

C. Carr allowed £ 4 5 s. 6 d.

N WHEREAS

J. Marſh allowed £3 5*s*.

WHEREAS Mr. *James Marſh* exhibited unto this Aſſembly an Account, by him charged againſt the Colony, for the Freight of Powder, intrenching Tools, &c. for the Colony's Brigade, ſtationed upon *Rhode-Iſland*, and for the Paſſage of Col. *Babcock* and his Guard from *Newport* to *Providence:* It is *Voted and Reſolved,* upon due Examination of the ſaid Account, That the ſame be allowed; and that *Three Pounds Five Shillings* Lawful Money, being the Amount thereof, be paid the ſaid *James Marſh*, out of the General-Treaſury.

A. D. Wolfe allowed £1 11*s*. 3*d*.

WHEREAS Mr. *Anthony De Wolfe* exhibited unto this Aſſembly an Account, by him charged againſt the Colony, for Plank and Timber by him ſupplied for the Fort at *Briſtol* Ferry: It is *Voted and Reſolved*, upon due Examination of the ſaid Account, That the ſame be and hereby is allowed; and that *One Pound Eleven Shillings and Threepence* Lawful Money, being the Amount thereof, be paid the ſaid *Anthony De Wolfe*, out of the General-Treaſury.

W. Lindſey allowed £4 9*s*. 11*d*.

WHEREAS Mr. *William Lindſey* exhibited unto this Aſſembly an Account, by him charged againſt the Colony, for Plank and Timber ſupplied for, and Work by him done upon the Fort at *Briſtol* Ferry: It is *Voted and Reſolved,* upon due Conſideration of the ſaid Account, That the ſame be and hereby is allowed; and that *Four Pounds Nine Shillings and Elevenpence* Lawful Money, being the Amount thereof, be paid the ſaid *William Lindſey*, out of the General-Treaſury.

W. Cole allowed £1 11*s*. 6*d*.

MR. *William Cole* having exhibited unto this Aſſembly an Account, by him charged againſt the Colony, for boarding and nurſing a Soldier belonging to Col. *Richmond's* Regiment: *It is Voted and Reſolved*, upon due Conſideration of the ſaid Account, That the ſame be and hereby is allowed; and that *One Pound Eleven Shillings and Sixpence* Lawful Money, being the Amount thereof, be paid the ſaid *William Cole*, out of the General-Treaſury.

June, 1776.

AN Account, charged by Mr. *Nathaniel Heath* N. *Heath* against the Colony, for boarding and nursing *Isaac* allowed £ 3 *Tyler,* a Soldier, belonging to Col. *Richmond's* Re- 7 *s.* giment, in his last Sickness, and for his Funeral Charges, having been presented to and duly examined by this Assembly : *It is Voted and Resolved,* That *Three Pounds Seven Shillings* Lawful Money be allowed and paid the said *Nathaniel Heath,* out of the General-Treasury ; which shall be in full Satisfaction of the said Account.

AN Account, charged by Dr. *Samuel Allen* against S. *Allen* al- *Isaac Tyler,* in the aforegoing Vote mentioned, for lowed 19 *s.* Medicines, and Attendance upon him in his last Illness, 4 *d.* having been exhibited to and duly considered by this Assembly : *It is Voted and Resolved,* That the same be and hereby is allowed ; and that *Nineteen Shillings and Fourpence* Lawful Money, being the Amount thereof, be paid the said *Samuel Allen,* out of the General-Treasury.

AN Account, charged by Mr. *Simeon Munro* against S. *Munro* al- the Colony, for boarding and nursing *Robert Morrison,* lowed £ 1 a sick Soldier, in the Service of this Colony, having 16 *s.* been laid before and duly examined by this Assembly : *It is Voted and Resolved,* That *One Pound Sixteen Shillings* Lawful Money be allowed, and paid out of the General-Treasury, to the said *Simeon Munro* ; which shall be in full Satisfaction for the said Account.

AN Account, charged by Mr. *Joshua Ingraham* J. *Ingraham* against the Colony, for the Rent of his House, Ware- allowed £ 5 house, and two Stores in *Bristol,* which were improved by the Colony's Troops, being laid before and duly examined by this Assembly : *It is Voted and Resolved,* That the same be and hereby is allowed ; and that *Five Pounds* Lawful Money, being the Amount thereof, be paid the said *Joshua Ingraham,* out of the General-Treasury.

AN Account, charged by Mr. *Gideon Northup* G. *Northup* against the Colony, for the Freight of Stock and Hay allowed £ 1 from 4 *s.* 8 *d.* ½ from *Jamestown* to the main Land, being laid before and duly confidered by this Affembly: *It is Voted and Refolved,* That the fame be and hereby is allowed; and that *One Pound Four Shillings and Eightpence Halfpenny* Lawful Money, being the Amount thereof, be paid the faid *Gideon Northup,* out of the General-Treafury.

Lindfey and *Wardwell* allowed £ 1 8 s. 10 d.

WHEREAS Meffieurs *Lindfey* and *Wardwell* exhibited unto this Affembly an Account, by them charged againft the Colony, for Work done upon the Platform of the Fort at *Briftol* Ferry, *&c.* Upon Confideration whereof, *It is Voted and Refolved,* That the faid Account be and hereby is allowed; and that *One Pound Eight Shillings and Tenpence,* being the Amount of it, be paid the faid *Lindfey* and *Wardwell,* out of the General-Treafury.

T. Sabin allowed £ 18 s 4 s.

AN Account, charged by Mr. *Thomas Sabin* againft the Colony, for the Board and Entertainment of the *Indian* Chiefs who were before this Affembly in *January* laft, being exhibited to and duly confidered by this Affembly: *It is Voted and Refolved,* That *Eighteen Pounds Fourteen Shillings* Lawful Money be allowed and paid to the faid *Thomas Sabin,* out of the General-Treafury; which fhall be in full Satisfaction for the faid Account.

J. Carter allowed £ 30 4 s. 9 d.

WHEREAS Mr. *John Carter* exhibited unto this Affembly an Account, by him charged againft the Colony, for printing Lawful Money Bills, divers Acts of Affembly, Commiffions, Proclamations, *&c.* It is *Voted and Refolved,* upon due Examination of the faid Account, That the fame be and hereby is allowed; and that *Thirty Pounds Four Shillings and Ninepence* Lawful Money, being the Amount thereof, be paid the faid *John Carter,* out of the General-Treafury.

The Heirs of *S. Ward* allowed £ 272 7 d.

WHEREAS Capt. *Ethan Clarke,* Adminiftrator to the Eftate of the Hon. *Samuel Ward,* Efq; deceafed, late a Delegate from this Colony in the General Congrefs, exhibited unto this Affembly an Account, by him charged

charged againſt the Colony, for the Services of the ſaid *Samuel Ward*, in the ſaid Capacity, from the 26th Day of *Auguſt* laſt, to the 26th Day of *March* laſt, being the Day of his Death, for the Wages of his Servant and Horſe-hire, for his Expences in going to *Philadelphia*, and during his Abode there, and for the Charges of his laſt Sickneſs and Funeral, amounting to *Three Hundred and Ninety-two Pounds and Sevenpence* Lawful Money; and deducted therefrom the Sum of *One Hundred and Twenty Pounds*, received by the ſaid *Samuel Ward* from the Colony: *It is Voted and Reſolved*, upon due Examination of the ſaid Account, That the ſame be and hereby is allowed; and that *Two Hundred and Seventy-two Pounds and Sevenpence* Lawful Money, being the Balance thereof, be paid to the ſaid *Ethan Clarke*, as Adminiſtrator to the ſaid Eſtate, out of the General-Treaſury.

WHEREAS it appears to this Aſſembly, by a Report of the Committee appointed to eſtimate the Damages done to the Eſtate of Mr. *John Baniſter*, by the Colony Troops ſtationed in his Houſe, that they have made conſiderable Waſte and Deſtruction; and this Aſſembly being deſirous of making a reaſonable Allowance therefor, but not being ſatisfied with the ſaid Report, *Do Vote and Reſolve, and it is Voted and Reſolved*, That the Sum of *Eighty Pounds* Lawful Money be paid to the ſaid *John Baniſter*, out of the General-Treaſury, towards the Damages he hath ſuſtained as aforeſaid.

J. Baniſter allowed £ 80.

IT is Voted and Reſolved, That Mr. *Henry Peckham*, for the County of *Newport*, Mr. *Thomas Greene*, for the County of *Providence*, Mr. *Pardon Tillinghaſt*, for the County of *King's County*, Mr. *Benjamin Boſworth*, for the County of *Briſtol*, and Mr. *Thomas Tillinghaſt*, for the County of *Kent*, or the major Part of them, be and they are hereby appointed a Committee to enquire into the Damages done within this Colony, by the Troops in the Service of the Colony, before the Act was made directing who ſhould be anſwerable for ſuch Damages; and that they make Report to this Aſſembly at the next Seſſion.

Committee to enquire into the Damages done by the Troops in the Colony's Service.

T. Water-
houſe allowed
18 s. 7 d. ¼

AN Account, charged by Mr. *Timothy Waterhouſe* againſt the Colony, for repairing a Number of Chairs for the Court-Houſe in *Newport*, having been laid before and duly conſidered by this Aſſembly: *It is Voted and Reſolved,* That the ſame be and hereby is allowed; and that *Eighteen Shillings and Sevenpence One Farthing* Lawful Money, being the Amount thereof, be paid to the ſaid *Timothy Waterhouſe*, out of the General-Treaſury.

Committee to audit the Accounts of the Committee of Safety, and the Commiſſary.

IT is *Voted and Reſolved,* That Meſſieurs *Nathaniel Mumford, Thomas Greene,* and *Gideon Mumford,* be and they are hereby appointed a Committee to audit the Accounts of the Committee of Safety, and of the Commiſſary of the Colony's Brigade; and that they make Report to this Aſſembly at the next Seſſion.

J. Northup
allowed £ 5
7 s. 4 d.

AN Eſtimate of the Damages done to a Houſe in *Newport,* belonging to *John Northup,* Eſq; by the Soldiers of the Colony's Brigade, having been laid before and duly conſidered by this Aſſembly: *It is Voted and Reſolved,* That *Five Pounds Seven Shillings and Fourpence* Lawful Money, being the Sum they were eſtimated at, be allowed therefor, and paid the ſaid *John Northup,* out of the General-Treaſury.

J. G. Wanton, C. Lippitt, and *W. Ellery,* allowed £ 2 14 s.

WHEREAS Meſſieurs *John G. Wanton, Chriſtopher Lippitt,* and *William Ellery,* who were appointed a Committee to eſtimate the Damage done, by the Troops in the Colony's Service, to the Eſtate of Mr. *John Baniſter,* exhibited unto this Aſſembly an Account, by them charged againſt the Colony, for performing the ſaid Service: *It is Voted and Reſolved,* upon due Examination of the ſaid Account, That the ſame be and hereby is allowed; and that *Two Pounds Fourteen Shillings* Lawful Money, being the Amount thereof, be paid the ſaid *John G. Wanton, Chriſtopher Lippitt,* and *William Ellery,* out of the General-Treaſury.

An

An ACT empowering the Members of the Upper and Lower Houses of Assembly to tender, to such of the Inhabitants as are herein after mentioned, a Declaration or Test for Subscription.

WHEREAS the great Danger to which this Colony is exposed, makes it necessary to use every Measure for detecting those Persons among us who are inimical to the United Colonies, and preventing their doing Injury to the common Cause:

Test-Act.

BE it therefore Enacted by this General Assembly, and by the Authority thereof it is Enacted, That all the male Inhabitants of this Colony, of Sixteen Years of Age and upwards, who shall be suspected of being inimical to the United *American* Colonies, and the arduous Struggle in which they are engaged, against the Force of *Great-Britain,* shall make and subscribe the following Declaration or Test, *to wit:*

" *I THE Subscriber do solemnly and sincerely declare,*
" *That I believe the War, Resistance, and Opposition,*
" *in which the United* American *Colonies are now en-*
" *gaged, against the Fleets and Armies of* Great-Britain,
" *is on the Part of the said Colonies just and necessary:*
" *And that I will not, directly nor indirectly, afford Assist-*
" *ance of any Sort or Kind whatever to the said Fleets*
" *and Armies, during the Continuance of the present War;*
" *but that I will heartily assist in the Defence of the*
" *United Colonies.*"

AND be it further Enacted by the Authority aforesaid, That in case any such suspected Person shall refuse to subscribe the same, it shall be in the Power of either of the Members of the Upper or Lower House of Assembly, in this Colony, and they are hereby directed, to issue a Summon, and call the Person so refusing before him, and make Enquiry into the Reasons of his Refusal: And if he shall continue such Refusal,

without

without giving satisfactory Reasons for the same to the Member summoning him, or shall refuse to appear upon being summoned, such Member shall issue his Warrant, directed to the Sheriff of the County where the Person so refusing shall dwell, or his Deputy, commanding him with sufficient Aid to make strict and diligent Search for all Arms, Ammunition and warlike Stores, belonging to such Persons so refusing, and to take and deliver the same to the Captain of the Company of Militia in whose District the Delinquent shall live, to be made Use of in Time of an Alarm, taking a Receipt of the Captain therefor; which Arms, Ammunition and warlike Stores, shall be appraised by two indifferent Persons, to be appointed by such Member so issuing the Summons, and be paid for out of the General-Treasury: And that such Member, so summoning any suspected Person, shall make Return of all his Proceedings, in Pursuance of this Act, to the General Assembly, at the next succeeding Session after his issuing any Summons.

PROVIDED nevertheless, and it is further Enacted by the Authority aforesaid, That in case any Person so summoned shall produce a Certificate from the Clerk of any Meeting of the Friends, that he is in Unity with that Society, or shall take the Affirmation directed in an Act intituled, " An Act for the " Relief of Persons of tender Consciences, and for " preventing their being burthened with military " Duty," he shall be excused from subscribing the said Declaration or Test.

AND be it further Enacted by the Authority aforesaid, That a Copy of this Act be inserted in the next *Newport* Mercury and *Providence* Gazette.

※※※※※※※

Guns, &c. to be returned to J. Greene and others.

IT is Voted and Resolved, That Mr. *John Smith* be and he is hereby directed to deliver to Mr. *Ephraim Westcot* Four Guns, Bayonets and Cartouch-Boxes, for the same Articles which are due from the Colony

to

June, 1776.

to Meffieurs *Job Greene, Nathan Franklin, Uriah Franklin*, and *Peleg Colvin*, taking the faid *Weftcot's* Receipt therefor.

IT is Voted and Refolved, That the Thanks of this General Affembly be and they are hereby prefented to *John Collins*, Efq; for his Services at the Continental Congrefs; and that his Expences to, at and from *Philadelphia*, be allowed and paid, out of the General-Treafury. *Thanks given to J. Collins, and he allowed for his Journey to Philadelphia.*

IT is Voted and Refolved, That the Committee of Safety for the County of *Newport* purchafe Two Hundred Spears, for the Batteries in the Townfhip of *Newport*. *Spears to be provided for the Batteries in Newport.*

IT is Voted and Refolved, That the General-Treafurer be and he is hereby directed to profecute Mr. *Silas Cafey*, for a Breach of Contract, in not delivering a Quantity of Salt purchafed of him by the Colony. *S. Cafey to be fued.*

WHEREAS the Militia of the Town of *Exeter* is fo numerous as to be fufficient for Three Companies: It is therefore Voted and Refolved, That the fame be divided into Three Companies: That all the Perfons living to the Eaftward of *Second River*, fo called, where it comes out of *Weft-Greenwich*, running through the Land of *John Joffelyn*, until it comes to *John Chapman's* Grift-Mill; and from thence Southerly, as it runs, until it comes to *South-Kingftown*, fhall compofe the Firft Company: That the Perfons living to the Weftward of the faid Line, and to the Eaftward of a Line beginning at the Highway that comes from *News-Neck*, fo called, and running from thence Southerly, as the faid Highway runs, acrofs *Black-Plain*, to the Ten Rod Highway; and from thence Southerly, as the faid Highway runs, until it comes to the Town of *Richmond*, fhall compofe the Second Company; and that the Perfons living to the Weftward of the faid laft mentioned Line, fhall compofe the Third Company. *Militia in Exeter divided.*

J. Crandall's Petition referred to a Committee.

Mr. *Joseph Crandall* having by Petition reprefented to this Affembly, That he is Proprietor of a Dwelling-Houfe and Half a Lot of Land, fituate in *Newport,* which Dwelling-Houfe is enclofed in the Fort now erected there; and prayed that Allowance might be made him for the fame : *It is Voted and Refolved,* That Meffieurs *Samuel Fowler* and *Gideon Wanton* be and they are hereby appointed a Committee to enquire into the Matters fet forth in the faid Petition; and that they make Report to this Affembly at the next Seffion.

Sufpected Perfons to be removed from Newport.

Whereas Meffieurs *Richard Beale, John Nicoll, Nicholas Lechmere, Thomas Vernon,* and *Walter Chaloner,* having been examined before this Affembly, and refufed to fubfcribe the Teft, ordered by this Affembly to be tendered to fufpected Perfons; and it appearing that while they continue in the Principles by them avowed before this Affembly, they are juftly to be deemed unfriendly to the United Colonies : *It is therefore Voted and Refolved,* That the Sheriff of the County of *Newport* forthwith remove the faid *Richard Beale, John Nicoll, Nicholas Lechmere,* and *Thomas Vernon,* to the Town of *Gloucefter,* in this Colony, where they fhall be permitted to go at large within the Limits of faid Town, they giving their Parole of Honor to continue there until further Orders from this Affembly : That if either of them fhall forfeit his Parole, he fhall, upon being apprehended, be committed to Gaol, and kept clofely confined until further Orders from this Affembly : And that in cafe either of them fhall refufe to give his Parole as aforefaid, he fhall be confined to fuch Houfe, in the faid Town of *Gloucefter,* as the faid Sheriff fhall think fit, with Liberty of the Farm whereon the Houfe ftands. And whereas the faid Sheriff hath in his Hands feveral Executions againft the faid *Walter Chaloner,* which are foon returnable, and upon which he is now in the Cuftody of the faid Sheriff : *It is therefore further Voted and Refolved,* That as foon as the faid *Walter Chaloner* fhall be difcharged from the faid Executions, the faid Sheriff immediately remove him to the faid Town of *Gloucefter,*

Gloucester, in Manner as the said *Richard Beale* and others are ordered to be removed, and under the like Conditions and Restrictions.

An Account, charged by Mr. *Samuel Anthony* against the Colony, for his Horse-hire, Time and Expences, in going Express upon public Business from *Newport* to *Dartmouth*, and from *Newport* to *Providence*, having been laid before and duly examined by this Assembly: *It is Voted and Resolved*, That *Four Pounds One Shilling* Lawful Money be allowed and paid the said *Samuel Anthony*, out of the General-Treasury; which shall be in full Satisfaction of the said Account. — *S. Anthony allowed £ 4 1 s.*

An Account, charged by Messieurs *William Dillingham* and *Fleet Greene* against the Colony, for a large Cedar Boat, taken by General *Hopkins* for the Use of the Colony, having been laid before and duly examined by this Assembly: *It is Voted and Resolved*, That *Eight Pounds* Lawful Money be allowed and paid the said *William Dillingham* and *Fleet Greene*, out of the General-Treasury; which shall be in full Compensation for the said Boat. — *W. Dillingham and F. Greene allowed £ 8.*

It is Voted and Resolved, That a Boat belonging to *George Wightman*, now in Possession of the Colony, be delivered to his Wife, to be improved by her, for the Support of herself and Family. — *G. Wightman's Wife to have his Boat.*

It is Voted and Resolved, That this Colony do purchase of Col. *Joseph Noyes* all the Salt that he hath to dispose of; and that he be allowed and paid therefor at the Rate of *Four Shillings per* Bushel. — *J. Noyes's Salt bought for the Colony.*

Mr. *Thomas Crandall* having by Petition represented unto this Assembly, that he is Proprietor of a Dwelling-House and Lot of Land, situate in *Newport*, which Dwelling-House is now occupied by the Troops in the Service of this Colony, and prayed an Allowance for the same: *It is Voted and Resolved*, That Messieurs *Samuel Fowler* and *Gideon Wanton* be and they are hereby appointed a Committee to enquire into — *T. Crandall's Petition referred to a Committee*

June, 1776.

into the Matters set forth in said Petition; and that they make Report to this Assembly at the next Session.

C. Child to al- IT is *Voted and Resolved,* That Mr. *Cromel Child*
low *N. Bowen* be and he is hereby empowered to agree with Mr.
for his Scow. *Nathan Bowen,* for the Value of the Damages done his Scow, while in the Service of the Colony.

Report upon WHEREAS Messieurs *Nathaniel Mumford* and *Thomas*
N. Miller's *Greene,* two of the Committee appointed to audit the
Accounts. Accounts of *Nathan Miller,* Esq; Commissary of the Colony's Brigade, presented unto this Assembly the Accounts of the said *Nathan Miller,* and the following State thereof, *to wit:*

Dr. *Nathan Miller,* Esq; Commissary, his Account Current with the Colony of *Rhode-Island.*

1776.
June 13. To Amount of Cash you received of the General-Treasurer, as *per* his Certificate, £14823 10 1
To Amount of sundry Deductions, 23 12 5
To Amount of 12,627 lb. of Hides, at 3 *d.* 157 16 9

£15004 19 3

1776.   Cr.
June 13. By Amount of your Account on the other Side, £12788 2 0
By short charged in Rum, *May* 24th, 2 0 0
By your Commissions on £12764 10 7, at 1 *per Cent.* 127 12 10
Balance due to the Colony, 2087 4 5

Newport, June 13, 1776. £15004 19 3
Errors excepted,
Per NATHAN MILLER.

Newport, June 13, 1776. This Day finished settling the above Accounts as stated.
NATHANIEL MUMFORD,
THOMAS GREENE.
N. B.

June, 1776.

N. B. Mr. *Nathan Miller* is to account with the Colony, for the Tallow he hath taken from the Beef belonging to the Colony.

NATHANIEL MUMFORD.

AND the Premises being duly considered, *It is Voted and Resolved*, That the foregoing Report be and the same is hereby accepted.

CAPT. *Samuel Carr* having supplied the Colony's Troops at *Jamestown* with Twenty-nine Pounds and Two Ounces of Gunpowder, and Eighty-four Musket Balls : *It is Voted and Resolved*, That the same be repaid the said *Samuel Carr*, out of the Colony's Stock. [Powder, &c. to be repaid S. Carr.]

IT *is Voted and Resolved*, That the Committee of Safety be and they are hereby directed to purchase every necessary Article for the Soldiers, Provisions excepted, and deliver the same to the Commissary, who shall supply the Soldiers with them at the prime Cost, including the Charges : And that a Bale of Cloaths, now in the Possession of Mr. *John Smith*, be immediately forwarded to the Commissary for the aforesaid Purpose. [Committee of Safety to furnish the Soldiers with Cloathing, &c.]

IT *is Voted and Resolved*, That his Honor the Governor be and he is hereby requested to inform the Delegates from this Colony in Congress, of the Act permitting Inoculation for the Small-Pox in this Colony, and desire them to move in Congress, as a Matter of real Importance to the Safety of the Army and the United Colonies, that all common Soldiers and Seamen, in the Continental Service, or who shall hereafter engage therein, be permitted to be inoculated at the Expence of the United Colonies, in such Hospitals as may be allowed, under such Restrictions and Rules as are or may be enacted by the respective Colonies. [The Delegates to propose to Congress, to permit the Continental Troops to be inoculated.]

AN Account, charged by Messieurs *Jonathan Jeffers*, *Samuel Brown*, and *Samuel Simpson*, for cleansing the Court-House in *Newport*, and cutting Wood for the [J. Jeffers, S. Brown, and S. Simpson, allowed £2. 8 s.]

the fame, from *June* 1775 to this Time, having been laid before and duly examined by this Affembly : *It is Voted and Refolved,* That the fame be and hereby is allowed ; and that *Two Pounds Eight Shillings* Lawful Money, being the Amount thereof, be paid the faid *Jonathan Jeffers, Samuel Brown,* and *Samuel Simpfon,* out of the General-Treafury.

N. Mumford allowed £ 15 15 s. 4 d.

WHEREAS Mr. *Nathaniel Mumford* exhibited unto this Affembly an Account, by him charged againft the Colony, for his Services and Expences, as one of a Committee in fettling the Accounts of feveral Members of the Committee of War, of the Commiffary of the Colony's Brigade, and divers other Accounts : *It is Voted and Refolved,* upon due Examination thereof, That the fame be and hereby is allowed ; and that *Fifteen Pounds Fifteen Shillings and Fourpence* Lawful Money, being the Amount of the faid Account, be paid the faid *Nathaniel Mumford,* out of the General-Treafury.

J. Jeffers and B. Wilbur allowed 17 s.

AN Account, charged by Meffieurs *Jonathan Jeffers* and *Benjamin Wilbur* againft the Colony, for mending the Windows of the Court-Houfe in *Newport,* having been laid before and duly examined by this Affembly, *It is Voted and Refolved,* That the fame be and hereby is allowed ; and that *Seventeen Shillings* Lawful Money, being the Amount thereof, be paid the faid *Jonathan Jeffers* and *Benjamin Wilbur,* out of the General-Treafury.

G. Mumford allowed £ 10 4 s.

AN Account, charged againft the Colony by *Gideon Mumford,* Efq; for his Services and Expences, as one of a Committee, in fettling the Accounts of feveral Members of the Committee of War, of the Commiffary of the Colony's Brigade, and divers other Accounts : *It is Voted and Refolved,* That the faid Account be and hereby is allowed ; and that *Ten Pounds Four Shillings* Lawful Money, being the Amount thereof, be paid the faid *Gideon Mumford,* out of the General-Treafury.

June, 1776.

IT is *Voted and Resolved,* That Messieurs *John G. Wanton, Samuel Fowler,* and *John Bartlet,* be and they are hereby appointed a Committee, to procure upon the best Terms they can a suitable House, to be used as an Hospital for the Colony Troops, stationed upon *Rhode-Island;* and that the Sick be immediately removed from the present Hospital, and the House be cleansed.

Committee to procure a House for a Hospital.

IT is *Voted and Resolved,* That *Daniel Mowry,* jun. Esq; be and he is hereby appointed to proceed immediately to the County of *Providence,* and make diligent Enquiry after the Persons concerned in counterfeiting the Bills of Credit emitted by this Colony: That he take with him the counterfeit Bill now before this Assembly; and that Capt. *Joseph Manchester* attend this Assembly, to give Information of what he knows respecting the said counterfeit Bill.

D. Mowry, jun. to make Enquiry after Persons who have counterfeited Money.

IT is *Voted and Resolved,* That Mr. *John Smith* be and he is hereby appointed and empowered to dispose of, at public Vendue, the Claret in his Possession belonging to the Colony; and that he give Notice of the Time of Sale in the *Newport* Mercury and *Providence* Gazette.

J. Smith to sell the Colony's Claret.

IT is *Voted and Resolved,* That Two Tons of Gunpowder be delivered out of the Colony's Store to Major *Robert Elliott,* for the Use of the Brigade stationed upon *Rhode-Island.*

Powder ordered to Newport.

IT is *Voted and Resolved,* That Col. *Henry Babcock* be and he is hereby allowed One Month's Pay, after the Time he was dismissed from the Command of the Regiment in the Service of this Colony; during which Time he was confined by the Pleurisy, with which he was seized while in the Service.

Allowance to Col. Babcock.

IT is *Voted and Resolved,* That Mr. *Nathan Miller,* Commissary of the Colony's Brigade, forthwith pay into the General-Treasury *One Thousand Pounds* Lawful Money, it being Part of the Sum by him taken

N. Miller to pay £ 1000 into the General-Treasury, and to purchase

Wood for the Troops. taken out of the General-Treafury, to purchafe Neceffaries for the faid Brigade, and now in his Hands undifpofed of.

A N D it is further Voted and Refolved, That the Commiffary of the Colony's Brigade purchafe Wood therefor, as heretofore.

✳✳✳✳✳✳✳✳

An **A C T** regulating Trade within this Colony, and eftablifhing proper Offices for entering and clearing Veffels and Merchandize.

Act for regulating Trade, &c.

BE *it Enacted by this General Affembly, and by the Authority thereof it is Enacted,* That any Goods, Wares and Merchandize, other than fhaken or knocked down Cafks for Melaffes, may be exported from this Colony, by the Inhabitants thereof, and of the other United Colonies, and by the People of all fuch Countries as are not fubject to the King of *Great-Britain,* to any Parts of the World which are not under the Dominion of the faid King : Provided that no Veffel be permitted to export any greater Number of fhaken or knocked down Melaffes Cafks than the fame Veffel is capable of carrying when filled.

A N D be it further Enacted by the Authority aforefaid, That any Goods, Wares and Merchandize, except fuch as are of the Growth and Manufacture of, or brought from any Country under the Dominion of the King of *Great-Britain,* and except *Eaft-India* Tea, may be imported from any other Parts of the World into this Colony, by the Inhabitants thereof, and of the other United Colonies, and by the People of all fuch Countries as are not fubject to the faid King.

A N D be it further Enacted by the Authority aforefaid, That there fhall be two Perfons annually appointed by this General Affembly as Intendants of Trade,

Trade, who shall be under Oath for the faithful Execution of their Offices; one of whom shall reside in and keep his Office at *Newport*, and the other shall reside in and keep his Office at *Providence*, and shall each of them be empowered to appoint a Deputy: That it shall be the Duty and Business of the said Intendants to take a Bond, payable to the Governor and Company of this Colony, to and for the Use of the Colony, from the Master of every Vessel cleared out at their respective Offices, with one sufficient Surety, in double the Value of the Cargo shipped on board such Vessel, conditioned for the true Observance of the Regulations made by the Most Honorable the Continental Congress, and this General Assembly, concerning Trade, and for securing the Observance of such Parts of the Association as are not inconsistent therewith; and that the Obligeor shall, within Eighteen Months after the Departure of the Vessel, produce to such Intendant a Certificate from the proper Officers, at the Port or Place where the Cargo shall be delivered (provided it be within the United Colonies, and proper Officers are appointed) or otherwise under the Hands and Seals of three or more respectable Merchants, residing there, that the same was there unladed: That the said Intendants shall also take Manifests upon Oath of the Cargoes exported and imported, and keep fair Accounts and Entries thereof, give Bills of Health when desired, grant Registers, shewing the Property of the Vessel cleared out (which Registers shall be also given under the Hand and Seal of the Governor of this Colony for the Time being) and sign Certificates that the Requisites for qualifying Vessels for Trade have been complied with: And that the said Intendants shall make Return to the General Assembly, at every Session, of all Imports and Exports.

AND be it further Enacted by the Authority aforesaid, That if any Vessel coming into this Colony shall break Bulk, before Report of her Cargo, and whence she came, be made to one of the said Intendants, the said Vessel and her Cargo, or such Part thereof as the

General Affembly fhall, upon confidering the Cafe, think fit, fhall be forfeited, one Half to the Ufe of the Colony, and the other Half to the Ufe of the Informer and Profecutor for the fame: And that if the Mafter of any Veffel fhall be convicted of having taken a falfe Oath before either of the faid Intendants, he fhall fuffer the Pains and Penalties of Perjury.

AND be it further Enacted by the Authority aforefaid, That all Profecutions and Trials, for any Offences againft the Regulations aforefaid, fhall be commenced and had before the Inferior Court of Common Pleas, in the County where fuch Offence fhall be committed; and that no Profecution upon any of the Bonds given as aforefaid, fhall be commenced after the Expiration of Three Years from the Date thereof.

AND be it further Enacted by the Authority aforefaid, That the faid Intendants fhall give conftant and regular Attendance in their refpective Offices every Day in the Year, *Sundays* excepted, from Ten o'Clock in the Forenoon, until One in the Afternoon; and fhall be allowed and receive the fame Fees for the fame, and fimilar Duty, as by a Law of this Colony were allowed to the late Collector of the Cuftoms in this Colony, until a proper Table of Fees fhall be eftablifhed by this General Affembly.

AND be it further Enacted by the Authority aforefaid, That all Goods, Wares and Merchandize, except fuch as are made Prize of, which fhall be imported directly or indirectly from *Great-Britain* or *Ireland* into this Colony, contrary to the Regulations eftablifhed by the faid Congrefs, fhall be forfeited, one Half to and for the Ufe of the Colony, and the other Half to the Ufe of the Informer and Profecutor for the fame, and fhall be liable to Trial and Condemnation in the Court erected in this Colony for the Trial of Prizes.

AND be it further Enacted by the Authority aforefaid, That a Copy of this Act be inferted in the *Newport* Mercury and *Providence* Gazette.

AN

AN Account, charged againſt the Colony by Mr. *J. Haſzard al-* *Jonathan Haſzard,* for his Services and Expences in lowed £3 7 *s.* going to *Block-Iſland,* by Order of this Aſſembly, to 6 *d.* apprehend ſome diſaffected Perſons, having been laid before and duly examined by this Aſſembly, *It is Voted and Reſolved,* That the ſame be and hereby is allowed; and that *Three Pounds Seven Shillings and Sixpence,* being the Amount thereof, be paid the ſaid *Jonathan Haſzard,* out of the General-Treaſury.

IT is Voted and Reſolved, That his Honor the Go- Committee to vernor, his Honor the Deputy-Governor, and the Aſ- act in the Re-ſiſtants of this Colony, Five of whom to be a Quorum, ceſs of the together with ſuch Members of the Lower Houſe of Aſſembly. Aſſembly as may attend, and the Secretary, be and they are hereby appointed a Committee to act and tranſact ſuch Buſineſs as the Exigency of public Affairs ſhall make (during the Receſs of the General Aſſembly) neceſſary; and that all their Acts and Doings be laid before this Aſſembly at the next Seſſion.

IT is Voted and Reſolved, That his Honor the De- Committee to puty-Governor, Mr. *Thomas Freebody,* Mr. *John* aſſign Places *Brown, William Potter,* Eſq; and *Charles Holden,* Eſq; for the Colo-be and they are hereby appointed a Committee to ny's Cannon. enquire into the Number of Cannon in this Colony belonging thereto, and to determine where it will be moſt advantageous to place them, and to give Orders for placing them accordingly; and that they make Report to this Aſſembly.

IT is Voted and Reſolved, That the following Of- Militia Of-ficers be and they are hereby appointed to command ficers ap-the Trained Bands or Companies of Militia in the pointed for Town of *Newport,* to wit: *Newport.*

William Tripp Captain, *Caleb Carr,* jun. Lieutenant, and *Jonathan Simmons* Enſign, of the Firſt Company.

Henry Wiles Captain, *Robert Dunbar* Lieutenant, and *William Pendleton* Enſign, of the Second Company.

Wing

Wing Spooner Captain, *Stukely Wyatt* Lieutenant, and *Lee Langley* Ensign, of the Third Company.

William Downing Captain, *John Nichols* Lieutenant, and *Benjamin Hammett* Ensign, of the Fourth Company.

Enquiry to be made for Guns taken from the Troops of this Colony.

IT is Voted and Resolved, That the several Members of the Committee of Safety be and they are hereby appointed and directed to enquire into and examine the Certificates of Guns taken from the Inhabitants of this Colony, while in the Continental Service; and that they make Report to this Assembly at the next Session.

Militia Officers appointed for *Exeter*.

IT is Voted and Resolved, That the following Persons be and they are hereby appointed to command the Trained Bands or Companies of Militia in the Town of *Exeter, to wit*:

Jonathan Bates Captain, *Stephen Wightman* Lieutenant, and *Henry Reynolds* Ensign, of the First Company.

John Hoxsie Captain, *George Sweet,* jun. Lieutenant, and *Eber Shearman* Ensign, of the Second Company.

Daniel Barber, jun. Captain, *Phinehas Kinyon* Lieutenant, and *George Wilcox* Ensign, of the Third Company.

Business before the Superior Court at *Bristol,* in *April* last, continued to next Term.

IT is Voted and Resolved, That all Actions, Matters, Causes and Things whatever, which were pending before the Superior Court of Judicature, Court of Assize and General Gaol Delivery, which was to have been holden at *Bristol* on the Second *Monday* in *April* last, but fell through, be and the same is hereby continued to the next Term of the said Court, to be then heard, tried and determined: That all Persons who are entitled to Executions from the said Court, which so ought to have been holden, have Liberty to take out the same; and that the Executions in Favour of *Cromel Child* against *Isaac Levi* be not stayed.

IT

IT is Voted and Resolved, That all Executions, for the staying of which Petitions are pending before this Assembly, be and the same are hereby stayed, until such Petitions be heard; and that this Vote be published in the *Newport* Mercury and *Providence* Gazette. *Executions where Petitions are pending stayed.*

IT is Voted and Resolved, That the Choice of Persons to Offices, which ought to have been filled up at the last or the present Session, be and the same is hereby referred to the next Session; and that in the mean Time the Persons sustaining such Offices continue to discharge the Duties of them, with as full Power and Authority as they have at any Time heretofore had. *Choice of Officers referred to the next Session.*

IT is Voted and Resolved, That all Business lying before this Assembly unfinished, be and the same is hereby referred to the next Session, to be then heard and determined: That the Secretary publish the Acts and Orders now made and passed, by Beat of Drum, in the Town of *Providence,* in Ten Days after the Rising of this Assembly, and within Thirty send Copies thereof to the Sheriff of each County in the Colony, by him to be transmitted to the respective Town-Clerks in the County: And that this Assembly be and hereby is adjourned unto the Third *Monday* in *August* next, then to meet in the Town of *Newport.* *Adjournment.*

GOD save the UNITED COLONIES.

Published according to Order, on Wednesday *the Twenty-Sixth Day of* June, A. D. 1776, *by*

HENRY WARD, Sec'ry.

A TRUE COPY, duly examined:

WITNESS,

PROVIDENCE: Printed by JOHN CARTER.

www.ingramcontent.com/pod-product-compliance
Lightning Source LLC
Chambersburg PA
CBHW020243090426
42735CB00010B/1817